Murder
ON THE
FLORIDA FRONTIER

$\mathcal{M}urder$
ON THE
FLORIDA FRONTIER

· · · *The True Story behind* · · ·
SANFORD'S HEADLESS MISER LEGEND

ANDREW FINK

THE
History
PRESS

Published by The History Press
Charleston, SC
www.historypress.com

Copyright © 2018 by Andrew Fink
All rights reserved

First published 2018

Manufactured in the United States

ISBN 9781467139397

Library of Congress Control Number: 2018948027

CONTENTS

Acknowledgements 7
Introduction 9

1. The Florida Frontier 13
2. Archie Newton 27
3. Becoming an Orange Grower 39
4. Samuel McMillan 50
5. Disappearance 68
6. Searching for Sam 83
7. Arrested 91
8. Trial by Jury 100
9. Getting Away with Murder 150
10. The Headless Miser's Ghost 157

Bibliography 165
Index 169
About the Author 173

ACKNOWLEDGEMENTS

Of course, no book of any sort is written alone, and this one is no different. I can't acknowledge and thank enough the staff at the Sanford Museum for helping me discover this story, research it and bring it to these pages. Curator Alicia Clarke and museum assistant Brigitte Stephenson were invaluable on so many different levels that listing them all would be impossible. So I say thank you.

There are many others who assisted me in researching names or tracking down people and places that have been lost to time. Andrew Mussell, archivist at the Honourable Society of Gray's Inn, was extremely helpful in providing information about members of the Inn, life in nineteenth-century English society and London in the 1860s. Miriam Gan Spalding at the State Archives of Florida rendered invaluable assistance in locating and reviewing the transcript material from the murder trial detailed in these pages. Adam Ware, historian and research librarian at the Orange County Regional History Center, and Bennett Lloyd, coordinator of the Museum of Seminole County History, both suffered my endless questions and inquiries and tolerated my visits, and for that I am grateful.

INTRODUCTION

*T*he shelves of the research room of the Sanford Museum are laden with all manner of books, binders, maps, folders, boxes, charts and more books. If you sit quietly, you can almost hear the wooden shelves groan and the reference materials cry out for more space. Or maybe I'm a little crazy and think I hear things.

It's not a large room to begin with, especially for housing the historical archives of a city that by Florida standards is among the older ones. And it must share space with stacks of chairs, crumbling city directories from 1889 to 1928, a copy machine, computers and several large museum artifacts that have not quite found a home yet.

It's among these arcana that I found the strange tale of Samuel McMillan and Archibald Newton.

Or rather, it found me.

Sometime in autumn 2016, while at the museum researching another book, I came across the story of the murder of a local orange grower, Samuel McMillan. He disappeared at the end of September 1882, mystifying friends and neighbors. Several weeks later, his headless, mutilated body was discovered in a nearby lake. Even though they didn't have any direct evidence, residents of the small, tight-knit community quickly accused a pair of outsiders, young Englishman Archibald Newton and his wife, Kate.

This was in a time when Florida was just getting its footing after the horrors of the American Civil War and the difficult period of Reconstruction.

Settlers, farmers, swindlers, opportunists and former soldiers from both sides were arriving in droves. Citrus production was in full swing, and as we shall see, Victorian ideals, mores and police work were in full effect. This also was the time of great capitalist expansion on this last of the great American frontiers, when, much like the American West, railroad magnates, land speculators and the Colt revolver reigned supreme.

As I dug deeper into this murder and its cast of characters, I was too intrigued to simply put it back on those crowded wooden shelves. Who was Samuel McMillan? Why did his neighbors accuse Newton? What was a young English lad from a wealthy family doing on the Florida frontier anyway? The information the museum had was tantalizing, but it scratched only the surface. Not one to miss a good story, I eventually put all the research materials of my initial book into a binder, closed it and focused on finding out what happened to McMillan and his apparent murderer.

"I think the Archibald Newton murder story was here waiting for you," museum curator Alicia Clarke told me early on. "I think he wanted you to find him and tell his story."

History has a way of doing that, of speaking out, of wanting to be told. And it often does so with a touch of the dramatic: I later realized that I had discovered this story and turned full attention to it on October 17—which is exactly the 134th anniversary of the discovery of McMillan's corpse (October 17, 1882). Cue the spooky music.

OK—so 134 years isn't exactly a dramatic milestone, and it isn't the round-numbered 100 or 150 years we normally celebrate, so spooky music may not be warranted. But discovering this story on the same day of the month the victim's body was found *is* dramatic, you must admit.

I also soon realized that I lived less than three miles from where all the main players had lived and worked in the 1880s. I frequently drove by the place where Samuel McMillan's house had stood, pumped gas at a 7-11 where his orange grove once blossomed and used the highway that now frames the events of this tale. In short, I had lived for ten-plus years at the epicenter of a century-old mystery, and didn't know it.

As I read more about the doomed McMillan and his accused killer, the more I became convinced this was a story that needed to be told. With events set in places ranging from the vibrant orange groves of Sanford, Florida, to the posh precincts of international financiers in London, the story has depth. In fact, our story originates even farther afield, in the Himalayan foothills of the extreme reaches of the British Empire at the height of its power. Throw in some poison, hordes of cash and a decomposing body, mix it all with Victorian detective work straight out of the pages of Sherlock Holmes, and we have a story worth reading.

Heck, there's even a ghost story for good measure.

This story also shows just how history can reveal itself. To tell this tale, Internet research was key for family history, maps, place names and so forth. But contrary to what many people think, the Internet doesn't have everything.

As mentioned, the staff at the Sanford Museum was invaluable. I also researched paper archives at the Seminole County Museum and the Orange County Regional History Center. I waded through twenty-plus years of reports and records of the Florida Land and Colonization Company. I enlisted the help of archivists at several institutions to physically search their records, including Yale University, the Florida Archives, Grays Inn of Court and a retired lawyer who claimed to have microfilm of every criminal trial in Orange County, Florida, from 1846 to 1913 stored in the attic of his cabin in North Carolina.

And most important of all, after much searching, I located the actual transcript of Newton's 1883 murder trial in a dusty, timeworn box among the shelves of the Florida state archives. The longhand script (no typewriters in 1883, thank you very much!) and the yellowed tri-fold pages of motions and court filings were a treasure-trove of information and enabled me to tell you this story. In fact, it's enabled Archibald Newton, Samuel McMillan, his friend Charles Saint, Edgar Harrison the coroner, Constable William Sirrine, Tony Fox, who found the corpse (and hauled it by rope), and all the participants to tell their story directly to you.

To this end, I've excerpted some of the testimony of the various witnesses in the original question/answer format. This dialogue comes from the transcript of the trial and comprises the actual words directly from the people involved.

One more point before we begin. I am a lawyer by trade. I'm not a historian (or is it "an" historian? I can never remember). But I was a history major in college and have always leaned toward the historical/archival/"wow it's so cool that happened so long ago." I'm known to buy old books at antique stores just because and collect fading photographs of people I don't know because they look distinguished.

Fortunately (or unfortunately, depending on your perspective), my college advisor was practical, and told me: "There's not much you can do with a history degree, Andy, except keep going to school. Law school would be best for you." So I did, taking a path into the law, where I've been ever since.

But this history mystery is a tale of murder, of inquests, evidence and forensics, and a sensational trial. In other words, perfect for a lawyer who loves history to share with you.

As you read, I hope you will consider the evidence and put yourself in the shoes of the prosecutor and the defense attorney in that sauna-like courtroom in June 1883. Sit in the jury box and absorb the testimony, pass Samuel McMillan's skull among yourselves and hold the bloody handkerchief. Put yourself in the wool suit of the twenty-two-year-old Archibald Newton, a British citizen hoping for justice on the American frontier.

Render your own verdict. Someone killed and mutilated Samuel McMillan—of that there is no doubt. But remember—Archibald Newton must be found guilty beyond all reasonable doubt.

1
THE FLORIDA FRONTIER

INDICTMENT

May 22, 1883. In a hot, stuffy second-floor courtroom packed with spectators, the clerk unfolded a tangle of crisp paper handed him by the judge and started to read the criminal indictment:

> *And so the jurors aforesaid, upon their oath aforesaid, do say that the said Archibald William Newton, the said Samuel McMillan in manner and form aforesaid, then and there feloniously, willfully, and from a premeditated design to effect the death of the said Samuel McMillan, did kill and murder, against the form of the Statute in such case made and provided to the evil example of all other in the like case offending and against the peace and dignity of the State of Florida.*

Sitting at the defendant's table, Archie Newton could not have fathomed how he'd ended up in a courtroom in Orlando, Florida, shackled and accused of brutally murdering his neighbor Samuel McMillan in October 1882. So much had happened, so fast, and he was so far from home.

He must have wished his mother and father were still alive to comfort him, give him legal advice and maybe even represent him. He certainly wished his brother-in-law had come to his aid by responding to his multiple letters pleading for help and for money.

But no one was there to help young Archie—except his wife, Kate. And she had been a murder suspect as well.

The list of charges ran several pages. Newton was accused of murdering his neighbor in several different and graphic ways: by pistol shot to the head (the lead bullet "penetrating the brain" and "inflicting a wound to a depth of four inches"); by beating him with his hands, fists and feet; by using "a stick" to inflict mortal wounds to the head; by throwing McMillan violently to the ground, causing grievous injury; by intentionally drowning McMillan in a local lake (Newton "cast, threw and pushed" McMillan in to the water until he was dead); and, with much finality, by slitting his throat with a knife to create a "wound of the length of four inches and the depth of three inches."

The courtroom was standing room only on this first day of the trial, filled with people anxious to get a glimpse of the twenty-two-year-old Englishman accused of such a gruesome murder. He and his young wife had gained much notoriety in the six months following his arrest and imprisonment. Threats of local justice were rampant, and papers had recently reported on a lynch mob being turned away by the jailer while trying to abduct another man also on trial for murder. It would only be a matter of time before Archie was next.

The crowd must have strained to lay eyes on his beautiful, somewhat mysterious wife, who would have been present at this court appearance. She likely was present at the murder—some even whispered that she had done it and forced her poor husband to take the fall.

Archie Newton was flanked at the defendant's table by his attorney, Eleazar K. Foster. He was an experienced, preeminent southern lawyer there to get Archie out of chains and onto the first train out of Florida.

But given the evidence—and Archie's past—prospects for freedom were dim.

The imposing Alexander St. Clair Abrams, known as the "Volcanic Creole," prosecuted this case. He fully intended to get a guilty verdict and see Archie hanged as soon as possible in a very public execution. With him sat Thomas Wilson, the former state prosecutor and a legal legend in his own right. Wilson lived a mere two miles from the scene of the murder and had participated in the desperate search for Samuel McMillan in the weeks following his disappearance. He even helped conduct the inquest and the initial criminal inquiry, which led to Newton's arrest. By his participation as a prosecutor, he now risked being called as a witness.

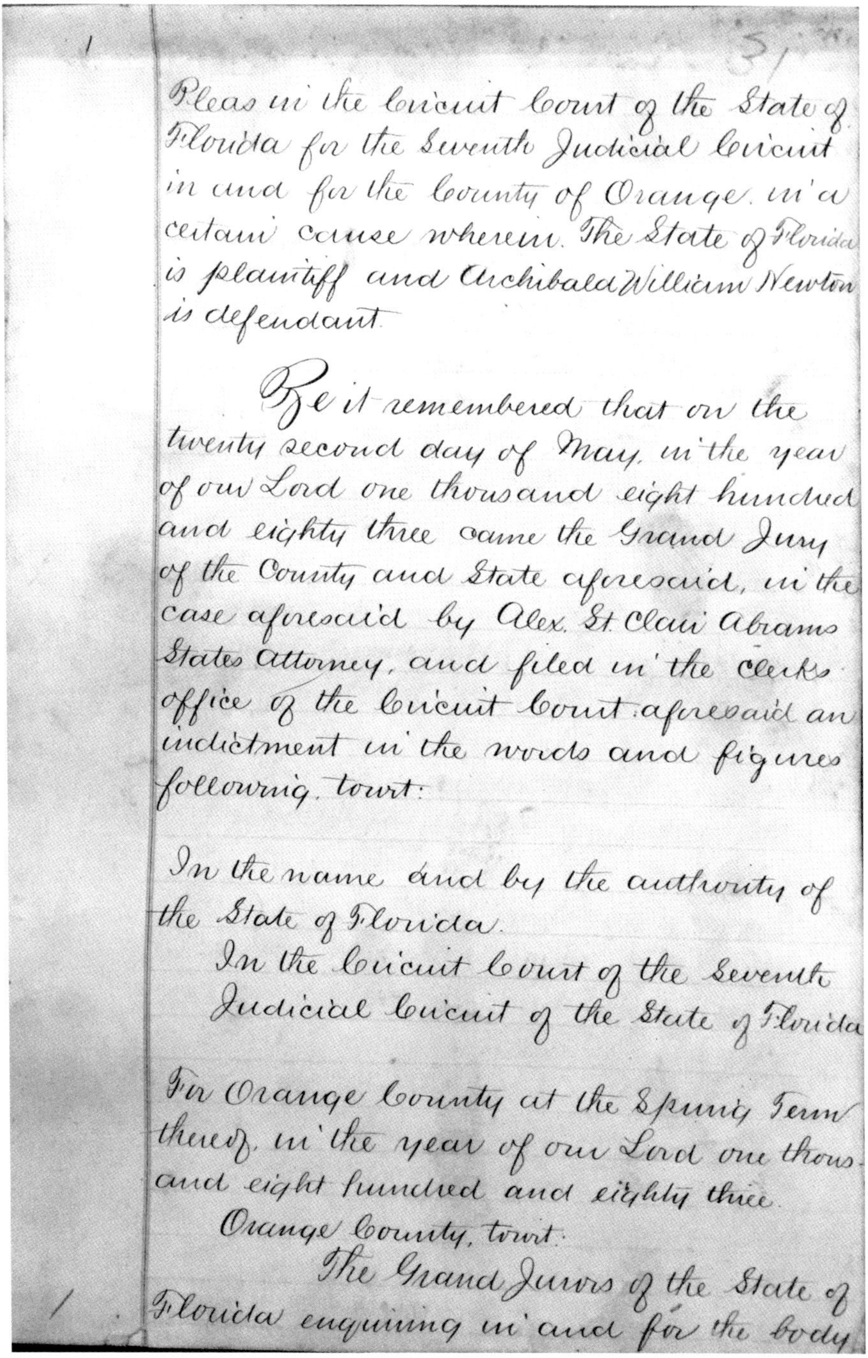

Pleas in the Circuit Court of the State of Florida for the Seventh Judicial Circuit in and for the County of Orange. In a certain cause wherein. The State of Florida is plaintiff and Archibald William Newton is defendant.

Be it remembered that on the twenty second day of May, in the year of our Lord one thousand eight hundred and eighty three came the Grand Jury of the County and State aforesaid, in the case aforesaid by Alex. St. Clair Abrams States Attorney, and filed in the clerks office of the Circuit Court aforesaid an indictment in the words and figures following, towit:

In the name and by the authority of the State of Florida.
In the Circuit Court of the Seventh Judicial Circuit of the State of Florida

For Orange County at the Spring Term thereof, in the year of our Lord one thousand eight hundred and eighty three.
Orange County, towit:
The Grand Jurors of the State of Florida enquiring in and for the body

Indictment for Murder in the First Degree against Archie Newton. *State Archives of Florida.*

As the judge banged his gavel on that hot day in May 1883 to get things started, Newton's lawyers abruptly stood and argued that all charges should be immediately dropped and Newton freed because the grand jury had been illegally assembled. The sheriff was questioned about his actions in finding jurors, lists were read, court was chaotic.

As the arguments raged and the motions were filed, the young defendant must have reflected back on how this all had happened...

AT THE CROSSROADS OF THE SOUTH

Archie Newton had arrived in Florida almost exactly two years before the disappearance and murder of Samuel McMillan. When he stepped off the river steamer from Jacksonville and made his way along the busy wharf of Sanford, Florida, he carried a letter of introduction from his wealthy uncle and a secret about his past—many secrets, in fact.

It was late November 1880, and he was looking for a new start, far away from his native England and the trouble he had gotten into just a month prior in London. It was farther still from the frontier of India, where he spent much of his childhood and where all four of his siblings had been born. In the span of one year, Archie had moved from one rugged, developing frontier in Bengal, India, to another—on the other side of the world—a rugged, developing railroad town of Central Florida.

But Florida would prove much more dangerous.

He had first set foot in America only a few days earlier, arriving in New York directly from London. With haste, he had boarded a passenger ship south to Jacksonville, Florida, where he switched to a river steamer and made the two-day journey into the interior of the state "discovered" by Ponce de Leon in 1513 and dubbed "full of flowers."

Archie had been instructed to disembark at the river port of Sanford and immediately present himself to James Ingraham, the authorized agent for his uncle's investment firm who would assist with arrangements for a new life. Ingraham was Newton's lifeline.

But like any good story, let's first set the stage before we bring out all the actors and set them in motion.

"RIVER OF LAKES"

Sanford, Florida, was, in November 1880, a bustling port town situated near the geographic middle of Florida. It sits snugly on the southern edge of Lake Monroe, about twenty-five miles north of Orlando and a mere thirty-five miles from the Atlantic Ocean.

Lake Monroe is actually less of a lake and more of a wide point on the long and winding St. Johns River, which originates in the marshland of the Everglades several hundred miles to the south. It served as resource, landmark, boundary and navigation route for the native peoples long before Europeans entered the picture. As the St. Johns flows north, it collects water from numerous marshes, swamps, small streams and springs. It also connects a multitude of lakes along the way, so much so that Native American tribes in this region called it Welaka, which means "River of Lakes."

The river takes many twists and turns before entering Lake Monroe from the southeast corner. It fills its 5-mile-wide basin to an average depth of about 20 feet and then continues its journey from the lake's northwest corner. The river meanders north for another 125 miles, eventually emptying into the Atlantic Ocean at the port of Jacksonville.

Originally, Mayaca and Jororo Indians inhabited this verdant area of Central Florida. The Sanford Museum has numerous artifacts on display from these long-lost peoples, including tools, arrowheads, burial goods and a fifty-foot-long dugout canoe unearthed from the mudflats during construction of a modern highway (Interstate 4). Several Indian burial mounds—a few of which existed into the late 1960s—dotted the southern shores of Lake Monroe.

By the mid- to late late nineteenth century, American settlers began braving the mosquitos and the heat to move into the interior of Florida. They used the south shore of Lake Monroe as the perfect disembarkation point. A fort was built, and a defensive road system stretched all the way to the Gulf of Mexico. These roads would later prove vital to the development of Sanford.

In addition to timber, citrus was the main cash crop in the Lake Monroe area. Although the first fruit-packing plant wasn't constructed until 1869, the area quickly became a primary source of oranges, pineapples, bananas, lemons, guava fruit and numerous types of flowers, all for export to the North. In the era before refrigeration, the shipment of fruit from South America, the Caribbean and the west coast of Africa was costly and wasteful:

in the late 1870s, as much as 60 to 70 percent of imported fruit rotted before reaching docks in Philadelphia, New York and Boston.

This made Florida's subtropical climate the perfect solution to the North's appetite for fresh fruit and vegetables.

By the time of Archie Newton's arrival in 1880, Sanford was the gateway to the whole of the rapidly developing Florida interior. Five different steamers arrived daily from Jacksonville, bringing passengers, finished goods, newspapers, mail and domesticated animals. Many of those disembarking at the Sanford docks were settlers hoping to build a new life among the oranges, palm trees and swamps of Central Florida.

The town's population was nearly two thousand souls. It already had four churches, three hotels, multiple dry goods, hardware and grocery stores, a fledgling school (whites only), two competing newspapers (one Republican, the other Democrat) and three saloons. Temperance (or, if you were on the other side, intemperance) was a hot topic at that time, and Sanford's saloons would soon become the subject of much scorn by a faction of religious groups. In fact, the intemperates may have been responsible for a devastating fire in 1887 that nearly destroyed the town— but that's a subject for another book.

HENRY S. SANFORD, STATESMAN AND LAND DEVELOPER

The town that Archie Newton saw in 1880 was founded by Henry S. Sanford, who purchased the land as an investment in 1870. He was attracted by the potential for citrus production and shipping and was betting on an influx of northern settlement and land sales.

He financed the initial layout of the town, the clearing of roads and the construction of the town's first buildings. He also financed promotion of the health and beauty of Florida and the wonderfully fair prices of acreage for sale. Land speculation was the name of the game, and Sanford hoped the droves of settlers would play and pay.

We must keep in mind that Sanford the town was started in the midst of post–Civil War Reconstruction, and it was located in the Deep South, which still mistrusted and resented northern interference. Sanford the man was the quintessential Yankee who felt entitled to make something in his own image: he was the son of a wealthy Connecticut tack manufacturer, educated in the finest boarding schools of New England, was fluent in

German and French and likely affected a cultured Brahmin lilt in his speech. No one would have been more conspicuously out of place on the Florida frontier than Henry Sanford.

How did he come to acquire this place? His father wanted him to assume the family business, and his uncle warned him about the temptations of travel and straying too far from home. But Henry Sanford had no desire to go into the family business and ignored the wishes of both his father and uncle. Good thing, as his life would prove that he was in fact a pretty bad businessman.

Instead, he traveled the world, forging a distinguished career as a diplomat, attorney, Civil War operative, investor and European dandy. He actually spent more of his life abroad rather than in the United States.

Henry S. Sanford. *Library of Congress.*

Although not a very good businessman, Sanford was skilled at international relations and, on some level, politics (although many historians feel that he was good at some politics because he was so unaware of his own shortcomings and inability to relate to people).

Either way, he carved out a varied and interesting career on the international stage. Not quite the Forrest Gump of his time, Henry Sanford was witness/participant to several important historic events.

He was an ardent supporter of the Union during the Civil War. Although he never formally enlisted or served in the military (and his wealth shielded him from being drafted), he used the honorific of "General" for much of his life. How? Like many high-born northerners, he made a donation in exchange for the honorary title. In Sanford's case, the Minnesota militia needed some cannons, which Sanford gladly acquired and shipped to become a general.

In 1861, President Lincoln named Sanford as the U.S. minister to Belgium. During the Civil War, Sanford supervised the U.S. spy network in Europe and is credited with securing gunpowder and other key supplies for the Union army, maintaining American influence in several courts and developing agents who thwarted Confederate spies trying to curry favor in Europe.

He later became confidant to King Leopold of Belgium and worked on his behalf (unsuccessfully) to secure U.S. recognition of the king's claims in the Congo and to promote American investment there.

GATE CITY OF SOUTH FLORIDA

The erstwhile general also invested in American growth and industry, buying large parcels of land in several states.

But the 12,548 acres (nearly 20 square miles) he acquired along the shores of Lake Monroe would become his legacy. Attracted mainly by the potential that Florida offered at this time, he purchased this tract in 1870. As Joshua Chase would later characterize it, Florida was "just emerging from the wilderness" at this time, and much work needed to be done.

In one of those ironies that history, with a sense of humor I think, often gives us, the seller of this immense land grant was former Confederate general Joseph Finnegan, who had purchased the tract several years earlier. Even though he did nothing to develop it, Finnegan was a good land speculator, as he reportedly made a tidy profit from selling to Henry Sanford.

Not one for modesty, Henry Sanford dubbed his new town Sanford. Since it was then the southernmost river steamer stop along the St. Johns River and the main access point to the rest of the state, he called it the "Gate City of South Florida."

In an attempt to find cheap labor as he developed his new town in the heart of Florida, Sanford imported groups of Swedish immigrants as indentured servants to do the backbreaking labor of building roads and starting what he envisioned would be a citrus empire in the subtropical wilderness. The Swedes were set up in a colony just south of the town in an area called Twin Lakes; their settlement was dubbed Upsala.

Sanford initially intended to develop a transportation hub on his new land based on river steamers. He built a 540-foot wharf out onto the water with a large storehouse at the end. Costing a whopping $2,970 ($57,000 in 2018 dollars), the wharf was intended to steal river traffic from the nearby town of Mellonville.

But Sanford's wharf generated little profit, and as in many business ventures, Sanford realized almost no return on his investment. Worse, the

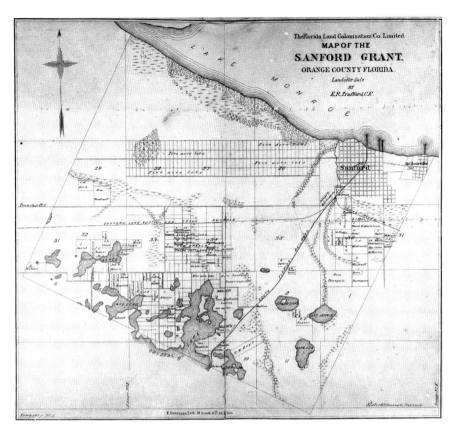

Map of the twenty square miles on Lake Monroe purchased by Henry Sanford in 1870. *Sanford Museum Collection.*

wharf lasted less than two years; it was destroyed when Lake Monroe flooded in 1871, ending its brief tenure.

But Henry DeForest, a shrewd businessman who had come to the Florida frontier in 1870 to make his fortune, saw opportunity in this disaster. He hired many of Sanford's Swedish labor force, salvaged most of the wood and built a new, larger wharf, which later proved most successful for DeForest and his growing business.

Sanford also started a wide-ranging citrus operation—named St. Gertrude's—just to the east of his new town, hoping to capitalize on the sales of fresh fruit to northern customers. But the land he chose for his groves was located too close to Lake Monroe and did not properly drain. He also failed to test the soil or take the time to understand the vagaries of growing citrus in the harsh Florida environment. Although much money and effort were planted, almost no fruit was harvested.

He eventually abandoned St. Gertrude's and established a new grove called Belair several miles outside the city. This was on higher ground in the Twin Lakes area, where the soil was much more conducive to citrus growth (and where, in an interesting twist, Henry DeForest had chosen his own land and built his home). With DeForest's help, Sanford built a sawmill and a lumber production company near Belair, which led to moderate profits for both men.

In March 1871, Sanford also teamed with DeForest to build and open a general store intended to outfit and supply the stream of settlers that was sure to follow. But the store suffered from periodic shortages of crucial supplies, and the liberal extension of credit eventually caught up. By March 1879, Sanford's personal finances were in trouble, and he was unable to continue propping up the general store.

In 1876, Sanford built the Sanford House Hotel to attract tourists and provide housing for wealthy visitors and would-be settlers to the city of Sanford. It faced Lake Monroe, and its landscaping included beautiful flowerbeds and citrus trees. A boardwalk led visitors straight from the hotel to the edge of Lake Monroe.

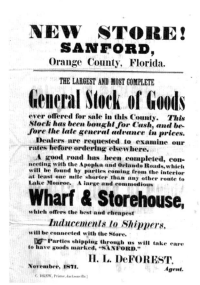

Advertisement for the Sanford General Store, opened in 1871. *Sanford Museum Collection.*

Even though the Sanford House Hotel would eventually become the social center of all major city events and celebrations—and Sanford often stayed there when he visited the town or entertained important guests—it was barely profitable. Guidebooks from the period included positive references and advertisements for the Sanford House, but the hotel failed to attract the expected flow of guests. It continued to make meager profits for the remainder of the nineteenth century.

When his direct business ventures failed or netted minimal return, Sanford latched onto railroad development as the next big thing.

As a port city with its advantageous perch on the main waterway into the

The Sanford House Hotel, a grand Victorian hotel on the shores of Lake Monroe. *Sanford Museum Collection.*

The grounds and lush gardens of the Sanford House Hotel. *Sanford Museum Collection.*

The train depot in Sanford, Florida, circa 1886. *Sanford Museum Collection.*

heart of Florida, the town attracted much interest from would-be railroad barons and opportunists. In 1879, the South Florida Railroad, which was building its line southward from Jacksonville, chose Sanford as its terminus for entry into the Florida interior and purchased land for its station. This was momentous news for Henry Sanford and his fledgling town, and he needed to promote it.

Using his connections to important men and his past service to the Union in the Civil War, Sanford was able to persuade Ulysses S. Grant to come and turn the first shovelful of dirt to start construction. Grant—war hero, two-term president and dark-horse third-term candidate—was perhaps the most famous American alive at the time and gave the Gate City and the railroad a much-needed boost.

A reporter from Jacksonville wrote in November 1883 that Sanford had become a "handsome little city, romantically situated on one of the most charming of our navigable lakes" and serves as a "Natural Gateway to this Section of the State." He also noted that Sanford is on a "latitudinal line with the Garden of Eden, that pre-historic en-closure wherein weak human nature fell, victimized by the machinations of the serpent."

THE BRITISH ARE COMING

Unfortunately, despite his connections to royalty, statesmen, famous Americans and wealthy financiers, Henry Sanford was in financial straits. In fact, by the time of Grant's visit in 1880, Sanford was struggling to pay his bills and teetered on the edge of financial ruin. This is how Archie Newton becomes connected to the Florida frontier, for it was at this time that British shipping scion Sir William MacKinnon entered the scene.

MacKinnon was a Scottish ship owner and businessman who established significant trade networks and commercial interests in British India and later in East Africa. Among other business ventures, he founded the British India Steam Navigation Company and the Imperial British East Africa Company. During his lifetime, he was one of the leading ship owners in the British Empire; by the 1880s, he controlled more shipping tonnage than any other individual in Britain.

MacKinnon met Sanford sometime in the late 1870s, and the two began corresponding regularly in 1879. MacKinnon's interest in Sanford initially stemmed from the former American ambassador's close relationship to King Leopold II of Belgium and his inner circle of businessmen, politicians and diplomats. Sanford, living in a château in Brussels, proved valuable to MacKinnon, who sought connections to support his expanding commercial ventures in East Africa.

Sanford proposed to MacKinnon a stock venture involving Sanford's Florida holdings. Sometime in late 1879, MacKinnon agreed to loan Sanford £8,000. Soon thereafter, he also agreed to "invest" in Sanford's Florida development activities by establishing a company for that express purpose.

The endeavor would be called the Florida Land and Colonization Company (FLCC); wealthy individuals would be found to invest in the company in exchange for shares. Profits would be generated from land sales, from the several businesses already in operation in Sanford and Henry Sanford's various other investments around Florida that were languishing.

The Florida Land and Colonization Company was officially registered in London on June 10, 1880, with its office located at 13 Austin Friars. MacKinnon's trusted advisors Edwyn Dawes and Archibald Gray were placed in charge. Gray was the nephew of MacKinnon and a successful businessman in his own right. They funneled the money to Sanford and would be important players as directors of the FLCC and the management of its affairs.

But almost from the beginning, there was serious friction between Sanford and the British board members. They mostly disagreed about business strategy, as Sanford frequently proposed initiatives deemed too bold or too risky for the British investors. Many of Sanford's schemes were not sound business practices anyway.

Keep in mind that MacKinnon had no ostensible interest in Florida or investing in land in America. He didn't give Sanford this large sum of money out of a bond of close friendship or an expression of belief in Sanford's business acumen. Rather, it was almost solely designed to keep MacKinnon close to Belgian leadership and promote MacKinnon's development schemes in Africa. He needed connections, and Sanford had them.

What does all this have to do with young Archie Newton and his alleged murder of Samuel McMillan, you ask?

Well, everything—Archie Newton was the nephew of Archibald Gray and great-nephew of the esteemed MacKinnon. They would soon make the fateful decision to send Newton to the Florida frontier—in which they had just invested—to get him out of England and away from the serious scandal he created.

2

ARCHIE NEWTON

ST. PANCRAS, LONDON

Unfortunately, much about Archibald William Newton is mysterious, starting with his date of birth. This was difficult to pin down because his birth record cannot be located, even though his parents were required under British law to register the birth.

Thankfully, his baptism record does survive. It tells us that he was born on March 18, 1861, in the St. Pancras district of London, England. He was baptized a little over a month later on April 21, 1861, at St. Saviour's Church in Hampstead.

According to the 1861 census, the family lived at 14 Queen's Terrace, Haverstock Hill. Archie is listed as a newborn son along with his parents, Thomas and Anne. The household also contained a "monthly nurse" (age fifty-six), a cook (age sixteen) and a housemaid (age thirteen) and an unmarried forty-three-year-old woman named Eliza Smith, who is listed as "sister," from Jakarta.

This snapshot in time tells us much about their circumstances and may help explain the familial context that would shape the newborn Archibald. The Haverstock Hill area of London was, in 1861, part of the rather large St. Pancras district. Queen's Terrace, where the family lived, no longer shows on maps of London; in fact, most of the other street names included in that particular census enumerator's schedule are lost to time.

This is because the Haverstock Hill area was about to dramatically change in terms of buildings, streets and living areas. While individual terraces such as Queen's Terrace still existed in 1861, they did not comport with the idea of "modern" streets intended by city planners and would soon be torn down.

Haverstock Hill wasn't a wealthy area but was intended for the respectable working class at the lower rung of the social ladder: small shopkeepers, clerks and tradesmen. The fact that the Newtons lived there, given the status of their respective families, suggests a newlywed couple making their first start with somewhat limited means.

A comfortable middle-class household would have had somewhere between two and six resident servants, and households exceeding that size were common. Although Archie Newton's parents listed three servants in 1861, one is a short-term nurse probably hired just to assist Archie's mother in her recovery. The other two are children (aged thirteen and sixteen), who would have been paid next to nothing for an exhausting workload.

THOMAS NEWTON, ATTORNEY

Archibald's father was Thomas Newton, born in Saugor, Bengal, India. He was the son of Major General Thomas Newton, who served in the Fortieth Regiment, Bengal Native Infantry, and is listed as serving in the British East India Company.

Archie's father was not a solider, however; he was trained in the law, qualifying as a notary public in "British Burmah" starting in August 1856. In colonial Britain, a notary was a less-qualified variation of an attorney, so the elder Newton was not quite a full lawyer. He served in this role until he journeyed to London in May 1860 to receive further legal education at Gray's Inn of Court and attempt to become fully certified to practice law.

But just six months after he arrived, Archie's father asked to leave and return to India as a fully certified lawyer. Since he had to complete twelve terms to be qualified as a full lawyer, his request was denied.

He returned to his studies and, over the next two years, completed seven terms. In January 1862, his second request to return to India with full status as a lawyer was granted. He said farewell to school, sailed with his wife and infant son back to India and established his own law practice in the Northwestern Provinces, likely in Allahabad. This is where young Archie Newton grew up.

ANNE GRAY MACKINNON NEWTON

Archie's mother was Anne Gray Newton (b. November 8, 1840), and her family was wealthy, well connected and would figure prominently in the destiny of young Archie. Anne's brother was Archibald Gray II, the same Archibald Gray of the Florida Land and Colonization Company. Her uncle was Sir William MacKinnon, the shipping magnate and a man of immense wealth described earlier.

This makes young Archie the nephew of a very wealthy and powerful financier (Archibald Gray II), and the great-nephew of an even wealthier and more powerful man behind it all (William MacKinnon).

Unfortunately, history does not tell us how Anne Gray met Thomas Newton. But we do know that her father was involved in the maritime trade in India and likely worked in some capacity for one of a number of William MacKinnon's far-flung shipping and colonization efforts. Since Thomas Newton was raised in India and had established a law practice there as a notary, it's not difficult to imagine their intersection and their meeting.

But we do know that she was only eighteen years old when she married Thomas Newton on April 1, 1859. He was thirty-six, twice her age.

A newspaper report of their marriage indicates that the union was entirely respectable from a societal perspective:

> *At Rangoon, on the 1st April 1859, by the Rev A Rose, Marriage Registrar, Thomas Newton, Esq, Notary Public, son of the late General J Newton, 40th BNI, to Miss Annie Gray, daughter of Captain Gray, commander of the S.S. Burmah* (Greenock Telegraph *and* Clyde Shipping Gazette, *June 7, 1859)*

Tragically, Anne died in November 1872 at age thirty-two; there are no records other than a notice of her death to indicate the cause. This undoubtedly had a tremendous impact on young Archie, who was only eleven years old when she died. In view of later events, we can see just how much of a loss this was for him.

But fate wasn't done with Archie yet. His father, Thomas, died in 1879, again of unknown causes and with little more than an official record noting his passing.

Archie Newton was then only eighteen years old and the elder statesman of his family.

"BOYISH FREAKS"

It seems that Archie returned to London in late 1879 or perhaps early 1880, probably after wrapping up his father's estate in India. By March 1880, he was living at a boardinghouse for gentlemen located on 154 Church Road in Islington, London, where fate once again intervened.

The house was run by a woman from Hull, England, named Charlotte Bowron. Two of her daughters—Kate and Pollie—worked at the house, cleaning, serving food and so forth.

Pollie would soon accuse Archie of drugging and raping her. Kate would soon marry him.

But before that extreme plot twist, we can reasonably surmise that Archie had turned to his Uncle Gray for help after the death of his father and to assist and probably relocate his family back to England. Later testimony indicates that Archie was a tea buyer in London at this time; perhaps Uncle Gray secured him a job at the London office of the British East India Company or hired him on at one of the companies that Gray, Dawes and Company either owned or invested in.

In this way, we can picture the nineteen-year old visiting the marbled rooms and gilded halls of Gray, Dawes and Company at 13 Austin Friars Lane in London, making supplication to his uncle and discussing his future. It seems that Gray established an allowance for Archie and undoubtedly gave him professional advice and letters of introduction. We would like to believe that Archie set about establishing himself in London, working hard and moving on from the tragic deaths of his parents back in India.

Alas, it seems that Archie did not settle in well in London. A paragraph in the local police intelligence section of the *Hackney and Kingsland Gazette* from March 3, 1880, reads as follows:

> *MORE BOYISH FREAKS (?)—Archibald Newton, 20, respectably dressed, calling himself a clerk, living at 154, Church-road, Southgate-road, was charged at Marylebone Police-court with willfully breaking a street lamp in Mansfield Road, St. Pancras. He was fined 30s and 11s the value of the street lamp, or 14 days.*

While this doesn't necessarily indicate a troubled youth, it does indicate youthful indiscretion. It may also inform of a young man newly arrived from the far reaches of the empire who had not yet recovered from the loss of his parents and was not settled into his new life.

It doesn't appear that Archie went to jail or got into serious legal trouble over the broken street lamp. Instead, he likely sought money and legal help from his uncle, who probably paid the fine and made sure the matter was smoothed over. Unfortunately, it wouldn't be the last time Uncle Gray provided such assistance.

CHURCH ROAD BOARDINGHOUSE

Amid the gentlemen coming and going at the boardinghouse at 154 Church Road, Archie caught the eye of not one, but both of the young Bowron daughters. They may have heard him recounting the tragic story of the death of his parents or regaling people at dinner about life in India and living in exotic locations on the Bengal frontier. They definitely heard him talk about his family connections in London (and abroad) and that one word that would have been music to the ears of the Bowron sisters: money.

We can confirm that Archie made it known that he received an allowance and expected to inherit a significant amount of money from his uncle. Kate clearly knew of this expectation, and it's reasonable to assume that her sister Pollie did too. Both sisters may have tried to secure a place in Archie's heart and a piece of this financial pie.

Keep in mind that Archie was the great-nephew of Sir William MacKinnon. For perspective on what Archie may have been expecting from an inheritance standpoint, MacKinnon's fortune when he died in 1892 equated to approximately $100 million in 2018 figures—a hefty expectation indeed.

Archie and the Bowron sisters would have had to abide by a very strict Victorian code for courtship. Acceptable male-female interaction would have been quite limited, and proper "contact" was at times difficult for young couples. Of course, we don't know what kind of interaction Archie had with the sisters or whether he or they observed social protocol. We don't even know if there was a courtship period or formal meetings under the watchful eye of Mrs. Bowron or another matron in her place.

But we do know one important earth-shattering fact: in October 1880, Pollie Bowron claimed to be pregnant. And she unequivocally identified Archie Newton as the father.

This is a serious charge in any time, but it was especially so in Victorian times. It would have required Archie to either accept the charge, acknowledge

MURDER ON THE FLORIDA FRONTIER

paternity and marry Pollie or work to disprove it. The latter course would require hiring a lawyer, gathering witnesses and presenting evidence as refutation. For a young man just arrived in London and trying to get his life in order, either course would have been devastating.

As I've mentioned, there are unfortunately no surviving diaries or other records written by either Archie or Kate Newton. So, recounting their side of this sordid tale is difficult, and I've tried not to draw conclusions that aren't supported by facts or other eyewitnesses. For this reason, Archie's brief time in London is framed by a few newspaper accounts and the testimony of a London housekeeper named Ellen Jones, who would later be called as the star witness in his murder trial in 1883.

WHAT THE HOUSEKEEPER SAW

Ellen Jones lived at 21 Kingsbury Road, a few blocks from the Bowron boardinghouse on Church Road, which she called a "very respectable neighborhood." Although she never set foot in it, Mrs. Jones walked by the Bowron house many times and said it was very nice from the outside.

This contrasted starkly with the Bowrons' financial background. Mrs. Jones knew them to be a rather poor family from Hull, England. Mrs. Bowron apparently had received a small amount of money after her husband died, and she had used this to buy the boardinghouse in London as a way out of poverty.

But she gave up in early 1881 and returned to Hull because the upkeep was too expensive, and too many boarders didn't pay.

Mrs. Jones kept her own rooms for boarders and performed various odd jobs in the neighborhood. This was how she came to know Kate and her sisters: Pollie, Emily and Nellie.

Kate actually lived at Jones's house from mid-July 1880 to March/early April 1881, at which time she returned home to Hull with her mother after closing down the boardinghouse.

In addition to helping to clean and care for the Bowron boardinghouse, Kate did "hat work" and other low-paying odd jobs such as sewing and cleaning. But such jobs were few and far between, and many times, Kate had no work at all and no money.

In what would become a key focus of the prosecution at Archie's later murder trial (which the courtroom listened to with "breathless interest" according to newspaper accounts), Kate Bowron was described as "wretchedly poor" and unable to buy even the most basic of clothing or necessities: Ellen Jones said "she had no clothing or anything." In fact, Jones felt so bad for Kate that she loaned her some of her own "under linens" because Kate's were in such threadbare condition. She also discovered, while walking with Kate in the rain, that Kate's shoes were no good. She gave Kate a suitable pair of boots she had received used and mended from her sister.

Kate returned this kindness by confiding in Mrs. Jones and sharing the gossip of her mother's boarders and the story of Archie Newton. Mrs. Jones didn't mention much about Pollie Bowron and her relationship with Archie, and she didn't provide any hint of a love triangle or competition between the sisters for the young gentleman's affections.

But she did talk about the dramatic confrontation near the end of October 1880 that led to Archie's downfall. Actually, Mrs. Jones was the host of the drama:

Q: Did Mr. Newton know of the financial condition of the Bowrons and was it ever the subject of conversation in presence by any of them and if so, what was said and when and where?
A: When Mr. Newton came to see me, I called his attention to their not having any clothes and he said he would give them one of his trunks and buy them some clothes, and Kate said she would not hear of it, they had some, but she knew at the time they had none, but would not receive it from Mr. Newton.

Q: Where did this conversation take place?
A: In my parlor in my house.

Q: About what time?
A: It was in the end of October.

Q: State whether any other conversations ever occurred in your presence and the presence of Mr. Newton and the Bowrons on the subject of their condition at any time?
A: Nothing more than about the clothes.

Q: Who were present at this conversation?
A: Me and my husband and Mr. Newton and Kate and her sister Pollie was there.

Q: What were the circumstances that led to the conversation?
A: Am I obliged to answer that question?

Q: Yes.
A: Her sister Pollie had had a child by Mr. Newton.

This revelation came during Newton's murder trial in 1883. It was an unexpected and spectacular story and caused much excitement in the courtroom. We can imagine the scene as the judge banged his gavel to restore order and the murmurs rippled.

Archie Newton, in London less than one year, had a relationship with a young woman at his boardinghouse for gentlemen and got her pregnant.

Mrs. Jones wasn't permitted to give more detail about the confrontation or the alleged paternity. We don't have the rest of the conversation or what happened after Pollie pointed the finger at Archie. We don't know anything about the child and can only surmise from the trial transcript that it had been born by October 1880.

Outside the courtroom, Mrs. Jones told a reporter from the *Cleveland Leader*, "His character was so bad that his friends had all forsaken him, and when we heard of this we were not at all surprised at the termination of his career."

With Pollie's accusation, the young Archie faced a serious criminal problem: seduction—or the "defilement of women"—was a crime.

CRIMINAL SEDUCTION

Stretching back a few centuries, English common law defined seduction as a felony committed "when a male person induced an unmarried female of previously chaste character to engage in an act of sexual intercourse on a promise of marriage." Historically, the female's father had the right to maintain an action for the seduction of his daughter, since this deprived him of services or earnings.

By 1880, British law had codified these principles in several sections of the Offenses Against the Person Act (1875), which spelled out the crimes of rape, abduction and defilement of women and "procuring the defilement" of underage girls.

The expression "illicit carnal connexion" was used in the law to refer to extramarital sexual affairs, and the age of the victim was critical, with harsher sentences for relations with a female under age twenty-one. Birth records from the Bowron family suggest that Pollie was not yet twenty-one when she met and was allegedly seduced by Archie.

If Pollie Bowron's allegations were true and Archie was the father of her baby, he likely would have been charged with defiling an underage girl (unless he subsequently married her). If Pollie were to suggest that their encounter was not consensual—which wouldn't have been a difficult next step—then a charge of rape would have resulted.

Since these crimes each carried a substantial term of either prison or penal servitude (potentially with hard labor), Archie rightfully feared for his liberty and his reputation.

He likely rushed to meet again with his uncle for advice and assistance of the legal variety. This meeting at Gray, Dawes and Company on 13 Austin Friar's Lane certainly wasn't as sympathetic or well received as the previous meetings, especially since this was at least the second time in just a few months that Archie was in legal trouble. While we don't have any account of this meeting, we know what resulted: Archie hastily packed his things and left London just two weeks later, never to return.

Curiously, it seems that on his way out, he stopped by Mrs. Jones's house at Kingsbury Road and bid farewell to Pollie. Kate was not present, and Mrs. Jones doesn't tell us what was said—or if any money or legal paperwork changed hands. However, given the apparent lack of an arrest or lawsuit, this meeting may have been some sort of payoff or contractual arrangement. Mrs. Jones did note that when Archie "went off he was very ill." He didn't write to Kate (or Pollie) for quite some time.

It's also possible that Archie delivered a bag of money to Pollie, and as part of the deal, the Bowrons had to shut down the boardinghouse on Church Road and leave London. Uncle Gray may not have wanted them around to besmirch the Gray or Newton families' reputations and would not have wanted an allegation such as this to touch the sterling reputation of Sir William MacKinnon.

There are no contemporary newspaper accounts or police records indicating that Archie was formally charged with a crime regarding Pollie Bowron's accusations. Archie's family connections were certainly impressive, and it was doubtless precisely to avoid this scandal that he was packed off abroad so quickly.

ESCAPE TO AMERICA

After Archie made his hasty escape, Pollie disappeared and the Bowron boardinghouse was shuttered.

But despite the allegations of her sister, Kate remained true to Archie. Indeed, the only surviving letter from Kate to Archie shows us how close their relationship had become by February 1881 and how angry she was about Pollie's allegations:

21 Kingsbury Rd
1 Balls Pond Rd
February 22, 1881

My Own dear Archie,

I received your letter and all your presents, for which I thank you very much indeed. I don't think there are many more people in London have anything like than you have. You know I have not got my ears pierced, but I shall have them done. As for the ring, it could not have fit me better if I had been measured for it. You may be sure I shall always wear it, and as to remembering you, I never forget you. I have had a letter from Nell and they wish to hear where Pollie is. So I wrote back and said they had better ask Bushell as I did not know. So Nellie is coming up. I don't care, I only wish all the nonsense was over. I suppose Pollie will tell a few more lies, but if she does, I know something about Bushell and her and if they don't mind what they say they will find themselves locked up for a few months. How my dear I have had no work for 6 months now and what is more I cannot get any, so goodness knows where I shall be just now, as I would not go to Hull if I was starving. I would prefer drowning to that. I paid Mrs. Jones 22 out of the money you sent me and when the other is done God knows what I am going to do then because I don't.

I sent you one _____, and am sending you another now. I put a penny stamp on them, I hope that is right. I was told it was. If you like you can send your letters here now not but that I always get them alright from Mrs. Fords. We have had no more cases of small pox and I don't think we shall now. Mamma was in an awful state for fear I should have it. I will close with all my love to your own dearself.

Believe me ever your own loving
Kitty

If I don't have a long letter from you very soon, I shall not write any more long ones to you. That will be an awful punishment, won't it.

Your own Kitty

This letter suggests that Archie had been in a serious romantic relationship with Kate, not Pollie. And it suggests both that Pollie may have lied about the pregnancy and that Kate knew it. This helps explain why one sister accused Archie of a heinous act and the other sister married him.

Kate returned to Hull in March 1881 with her mother, abruptly packing her few possessions and leaving London. Mrs. Jones wasn't there when she left, but she said that Kate left a letter on the mantelpiece and a one-pound note for the rent that she owned. Mrs. Jones said Archie sent the money so that Kate could pay her bill.

In the months between November 1880 and May 1881, Archie sent Kate money, letters and some jewelry—a brooch, earrings and rings. Jones described the earrings as "buffalo teeth," which she saw "a lot of" when she later came to America to testify at the trial. She also thought that Archie sent alligator teeth, which seemed to have been a novelty for Londoners.

Kate was extremely unhappy in Hull and seethed about her sister's allegations. She wrote to Mrs. Jones on April 12, 1881, and said that it was "miserable being at home" and that she had no work to do.

By late May 1881, Kate had had enough. She again wrote to Mrs. Jones that she "thanks goodness I have got all my money to go west." She was going to America to be with Archie. She disclosed her travel schedule and asked to stay with Mrs. Jones for a night or two. She also made the following tantalizing comment: "I have had a letter from Pollie and she says John has broken a blood vessel and is very ill. I will close, tell you all when I see you."

"John" may be the Bushell referred to in the earlier letter, and Pollie might have been living with or married to him. It also may suggest, although this is not verified, that the accusations against Archie were either false or that Pollie had received a sufficient payoff to move on.

Whatever the case, Kate left her family in Hull and returned to Mrs. Jones's house in London. She told Jones that she was going to America to marry Archie despite the allegations of her sister Pollie. Archie had promised to meet her in New York, marry her and take her to his new home in Florida. Flashing perhaps a darker side—or perhaps just a side that was weary of poverty and gossip—Kate told Mrs. Jones that "she would get her keep if she did not get anything else." She also said that "it would take £30 to get her to America, and she got that" from Newton to make the trip.

Still, Kate was desperately poor—so much so that she had to pawn some of the jewelry Newton had sent her (netting ten shillings) on several occasions just to get by. In fact, the day before her departure for America, she told Mrs. Jones that she didn't even have enough money to send a telegraph to Archie to tell him she was coming. And Mrs. Jones never saw any trunks, crates or luggage, which one would expect for such a life-changing journey to another country.

As she testified about these goings-on, it is clear that Ellen Jones thought very kindly of Kate Bowron, despite the scandal, the family drama and Kate's destitution. She commented several times that although rather poor, Kate was "very well behaved" and never caused any trouble. She also apparently didn't blame Kate or Archie for Pollie's accusations: "I only blame her for keeping up with Newton under the circumstances relating to her sister, that's all. If it was true of Newton, they say it was. Newton said it was not, she said it was not, the girl herself said it was."

In London, Kate scraped together enough money to send a telegram from the Dalston Lane Station. Sister Nellie took her to the Albert Docks, and Kate left England, never to return.

Archie wanted Kate to put "Mrs. Newton" on her travel papers when she came to America. He apparently wanted her to sail as a married woman (even though they were not yet married), perhaps for safety reasons. But Kate, showing a strong confident side despite her circumstances, told Mrs. Jones just before she left that she did not want to do this and instead would travel as herself.

And she did just that: ship records show an entry for "Kate Bowron" age twenty, "spinster," sailing alone in steerage aboard the steamer *The Greece*. It arrived in New York on June 23, 1881.

3
BECOMING AN ORANGE GROWER

ARCHIE'S ARRIVAL

Eight months before Kate crossed the Atlantic to join him, Archie Newton arrived in Florida. As instructed, he located and met with James Ingraham on November 25, 1880, and arrangements were made for the young Englishman to start his new life in Sanford, Florida.

Described as among the "group of men of great vision, determination and enterprise who molded the destiny of Florida" by the *St. Augustine Evening Record* of October 27, 1924, James Ingraham had been hired by Henry Sanford in 1874 to serve as manager of his new city's development. In this capacity, Ingraham is credited with organizing most of the early public works projects, laying out the streets and transportation routes and overseeing many of the early buildings. As he worked, Ingraham did his best to inject practicality and business acumen into the ideas and wishes thrown at him by absentee owner Henry Sanford, which would have been a mighty challenge indeed.

Ingraham traveled the United States extensively on Sanford's behalf, extolling the virtues of life in Florida generally and the benefit of investing or buying land in Sanford specifically. He and his wife and two children lived on a fifty-acre parcel a few miles south of Sanford called the Oaks, where he also managed a successful orange grove.

Above: Part of downtown Sanford, Florida, 1882. *Sanford Museum Collection.*

Right: James Ingraham. *Chase Collection, University of Florida.*

Ingraham would later work for business tycoon Henry Plant as president of the South Florida Railroad, expanding the line from Sanford all the way to Tampa. After that success, Ingraham became vice president of the Florida East Coast Railway, owned by another tycoon, Henry Flagler. Together, these two men were responsible for developing the entire east coast of Florida in the late nineteenth century.

The *Sanford Herald* wrote in January 1922 that even in old age, "he [Ingraham] is fondly remembered by many of the old timers as one of the best looking men in this part of Florida in the early days."

This was the force of a man that nineteen-year-old Archie Newton, on the run from trouble in London, met in November 1880.

Unfortunately, we don't have a diary from either Ingraham or Newton to know the details of their initial meeting or the first few weeks in Sanford. Ingraham made little reference to Archie Newton or the efforts he made on the younger man's behalf. It's possible that Ingraham wanted to forget the whole sordid affair and either didn't write about the events or later removed them from his papers. It's also possible that he excised such materials in preparation for the murder trial in 1883, to limit his own testimony, or that he turned them over to Newton's defense attorney.

Whatever the case, it doesn't appear that Ingraham was overly impressed with Archie. He only briefly mentioned their November meeting in a letter to Henry Sanford and thereafter provided mostly concise, factual updates in a businesslike tone about Newton.

Gray had directed Ingraham to receive his young nephew and get him established in Sanford. Ingraham said that he had been "instructed by the Secretary of the Company to make monthly payment to him on account of his uncle." Other than that, Ingraham later said that his instructions really weren't that specific:

> *Q: When Mr. Newton came out with the letter of introduction to you, did you or* [did you] *not receive from England any letters of instruction concerning him?*
> *A: Nothing particular except that I should give him such aid as I could, that he was desirous of locating on the grant or in the county, but I was not to influence him in his purchase, but if he found a place on the Grant he liked, to locate him. Otherwise, I was not to interfere in his affairs but to pay him money.*

Ingraham was ordered to pay Newton an allowance of about $83 a month, which equates to approximately $2,050 in 2018 dollars. According to Ingraham, the directors of the FLCC were very specific in this regard and told him that anything over this amount would be Ingraham's personal responsibility.

The first payment was made to Archie on November 29, 1880. The money earmarked for him was funneled to an account at the Philadelphia-based Manayoak Bank, which was accessible by Ingraham in his capacity as agent of FLCC. Commencement of this allowance would have been a godsend to the young Englishman, especially given the whirlwind few weeks he had just endured and what likely would have been a need for money.

"A SUITABLE PIECE OF LAND ON THE GRANT"

They wasted no time in searching for property for Archie to buy. After all, Ingraham had been dealing Florida real estate for more than five years. Letters he wrote to Henry Sanford indicate that Newton looked at several parcels of land in December and January but had not made a decision as to where to settle.

Uncle Gray wrote in February 1881 that he and the board wished Archie to find a "suitable piece of land on the Grant" to start his new life. Purchase of the land would count as a sale to the company and help bolster already-flagging sales. They also were undoubtedly interested in the investment potential, since the land could be resold later for a profit.

Archie found his ideal spot in January 1881. It was a prime parcel a few miles south of downtown Sanford, in the desirable Twin Lakes area. It was a half a mile from the Belair stop on the South Florida Railroad, which had recently started service to Orlando and would soon run all the way to Tampa on the Gulf of Mexico.

A down payment of $50 was made on January 31, 1881, to secure the lot. It seems that Newton may have put a contingent offer on the land in December, as he continued to look at other properties before making a final decision. Ingraham's ledger book shows the following entry: "To A.W. Newton on order of DeForest for payment on land to hold same—order given Dec 10th $50.00 Sanford."

The seller was none other than Henry DeForest, who seemed to have the magic touch when it came to business and development in and around Sanford.

Henry DeForest. *Sanford Museum Collection.*

In fact, this parcel was just down the road from DeForest's own large house and near the Sanford Mill, which DeForest had led to profitability and was supplying much of the finished lumber products for the whole area.

It was an area of rich soil and good drainage, where many successful groves had been producing large yields of oranges and other prime crops: lemons, dates, figs, pomegranates, guava, bananas and pineapples. Numerous landowners were making significant profits growing fruit and shipping it north to ready consumers. This had been Henry Sanford's original hope in 1871—to grow citrus and take advantage of the strategic position of the town as a transportation hub—and was one of the prime reasons he acquired the land in this area in the first place. It was now beginning to bear fruit, literally and figuratively.

Archie Newton closed the deal on March 19, 1881, just as Kate Bowron was helping her mother close down the London boardinghouse and retreat to Hull. So, a little over three months after arriving in Florida and a little over four months after being accused of seducing Pollie Bowron, Archie Newton bought ten acres of land on the Florida frontier. Or rather, his uncle bought it for him. The recorded deed lists the buyers as Edwin Sandys Dawes and Archibald Gray, who acquired the land for the substantial price of $1,500. Henry DeForest booked a substantial profit, having bought the land a few years before for only $500.

The plot was located on the south side of Eureka Avenue, the main east–west thoroughfare through the Twin Lakes area that connected it with a town called Paola two miles to the west and to the outskirts of Sanford several miles to the east. The road crossed gentle rolling hills and open meadows and was well suited for cultivating orange trees. In addition to passing between the Upper and Lower Twin Lakes for which the area was named, Eureka Avenue bordered Lake Como and the attached Crystal Lake, which will figure prominently in our story.

A quirk of plat divisions of years past, Archie's parcel didn't have direct access to Eureka Avenue—so the deed included a long right-of-way in the

Sale of land for Archie Newton's new home. *Sanford Museum Collection.*

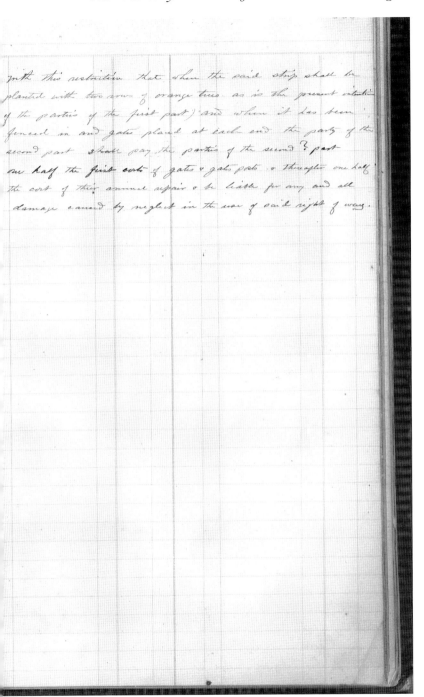

with this restriction that when the said strip shall be
planted with two rows of orange trees as is the present intention
of the parties of the first part) and when it has been
fenced in and gates placed at each end the party of the
second part shall pay the parties of the second part
one half the first cost of gates & gate posts & thereafter one half
the cost of their annual repair & be liable for any and all
damage caused by neglect in the use of said right of way.

House owned by wealthy Boston native Charles Amory, a few doors from Archie Newton's new home. *Sanford Museum Collection.*

northwest corner through his neighbor's lot for access to the road, as long as two rows of orange trees were planted on this portion and a fence with a gate at each end was erected.

Ingraham was a witness to the deed, and as soon as the ink was dry, he immediately helped Archie put in motion the necessary arrangements for building a house. Payments for clearing the land commenced as soon as March 23 and continued for the next several weeks.

Throughout April and May, purchases were made for fencing, lumber, tools, dry goods, stovepipe, hauling and labor. Most of these supplies were purchased from Henry DeForest, his Sanford Mill and the hardware store of W.J. Hill (where Newton had a running account). Shingles were paid for on May 31, suggesting that the house was up and roofing was underway.

Archie ended up building a two-story house, a barn and a small shed at the back of the property. It had a dock on Lake Como, to which a rowboat was usually tied. (This rowboat—scrubbed clean—would later be mentioned with suspicion in McMillan's disappearance and murder.) From various statements and testimony, we know the front of the house faced north and was lined with a large porch. A pathway (also described as a "road," a "wagon path" and the main entrance to the house) led out from the northwest corner of the house on its long stretch to Eureka Avenue.

About seventy-five feet from the house, down the main driveway, a footpath turned off to the west and cut through acres of orange trees and undeveloped woods. Several locals called this pathway the "Old Apopka Road" and the "Sanford Road," although it appears it was little more than a pathway through the trees for horses and people. It wasn't large enough or clear enough for wagons. More importantly for our story, this path led directly to the property of Samuel McMillan, whose fateful meeting with Archie Newton is the subject of this story. Indeed, a little over a year and a half later, it was the last place McMillan was seen alive.

The first floor of the Newton house had a front room for receiving and a formal parlor in the back of the house, which was the south side. There was a large sofa on the north wall of the parlor, and windows affording

Typical style of house in the Paola/Twin Lakes area, circa 1880. Archie Newton's house would likely have been built in a similar style. *Sanford Museum Collection.*

sweeping views of the lake lined the back of the room. Two bedrooms were located upstairs.

We know that Kate Bowron arrived in America on June 23, 1881. It therefore appears that Archie was able to get the house almost completely built in time for him to travel to New York City, meet Kate, marry her and return to their new home in Florida.

This timeline is confirmed by two important home improvements that every new husband would do well to remember: paint color and furniture. These two items were not purchased for the Newton home until mid-July 1881. This gave the newlyweds time to return, move in and make these important decisions together.

Ingraham kept tabs on the house construction but later said he didn't involve himself beyond paying Archie's monthly allowance and disbursing other drafts and bank orders drawn by Newton to pay for the construction. Given Newton's age and relative inexperience with such matters, Ingraham may have lent more of a helping hand than he indicated, but he may have been trying to distance himself from Archie by the time of the murder trial in June 1883.

We can only speculate how Ingraham actually felt about all this. An industrious, hardworking businessman, Ingraham had been forced to

Henry DeForest's home in Twin Lakes. *Sanford Museum Collection.*

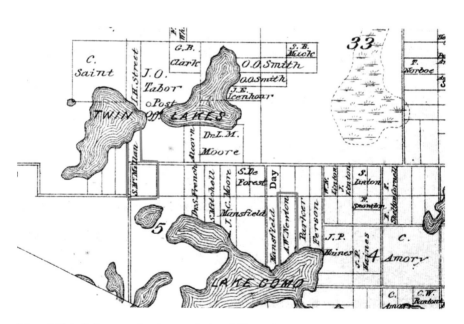

Map of Twin Lakes area showing proximity of Newton's home and McMillan's orange grove. *Sanford Museum Collection.*

manage the affairs of the nineteen-year-old nephew of his foreign employer and pay him a generous allowance each month. He facilitated the search for land, drew up the deed for his English masters to sign, handled their money and made sure a large house and barn were finished. It certainly wouldn't have seemed fair to him or most of the other industrious people carving a living in the heat and swamps of the Florida frontier at this time.

Ingraham was instructed to pay Archie an additional allowance of $250 that summer to cover extra expenses for furniture, tools and the establishment of an orange grove. There are numerous entries on the company's books throughout the latter part of 1881 and into 1882 for trees, farm implements and manure, the most important tool of all when starting an orange grove.

It seems that Archie really intended to settle down and make a go of planting and growing fruit. All he had to do now was manage his newly planted orange trees, settle in with his new wife and stay out of trouble.

But that's when he met Samuel McMillan.

4

SAMUEL McMILLAN

THE MISER

Samuel McMillan came from a much humbler background and had arrived on the Florida frontier under significantly different circumstances than his accused killer Archibald Newton.

He was born in 1835 in Columbiana County, Ohio, a hardworking area in the mid-northeastern corner of the state near the Pennsylvania border. He spent his childhood in the town of Salem; in light of McMillan's eventual ghastly demise, conspiracy theorists and ghost hunters may delight at this "connection" to the infamous town in Massachusetts.

As a teenager, McMillan worked in the printing office of the *Salem Republican* newspaper. He worked there until about age twenty, at which time he left to pursue his fortune. He leased a nearby tract of land and established a coalmine. At that time, coal was a profitable commodity and much in demand, and since he lived in the heart of coal country, this was certainly a perfect venture to pursue.

An article in the January 30, 1884 *Cleveland Leader* noted that by McMillan's "careful management and well-known business tact, the venture proved a success, and in time he acquired considerable property."

In 1874, McMillan's health "became impaired," and he decided to relocate and recuperate "in the salubrious climate of Florida." During this time, a number of Ohio natives were moving south and purchased land in and around the Twin Lakes/Paola area. Many of these settlers hailed from

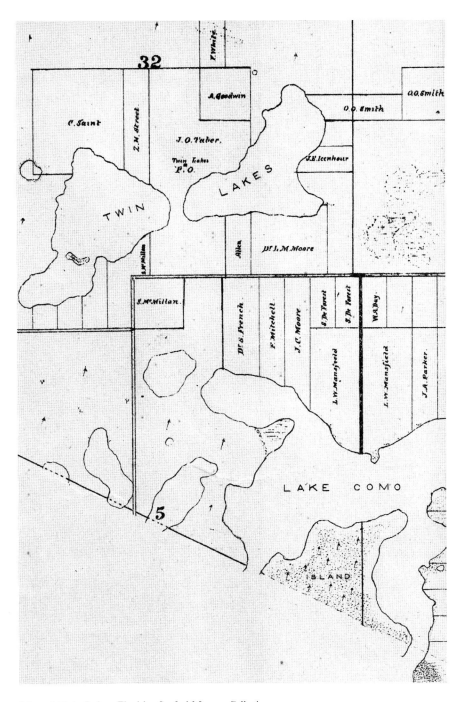

Map of Twin Lakes, Florida. *Sanford Museum Collection.*

Salem, Ohio; Sam probably saw advertisements for this venture and heard testimonials about the fine climate and may have decided to head south to build on his fortune.

He purchased a little over fifteen acres of land right on Twin Lakes, near several other expats from Salem, many of whom he had known back in Ohio. He cleared the land, fenced it in and planted a large orange grove. Newspaper accounts indicate that when the trees reached maturity, the grove "became profitable and realized a considerable sum of money at certain seasons of the year."

Not one to rest on what he had, McMillan invested in several other parcels of land on the Florida frontier, one located approximately fifteen miles to the south near a small crossroads village called Orlando and another in Deland in Volusia County about fifteen miles to the north. By all accounts, each of these lots also produced fine yields of citrus and profits for Samuel.

Based on the testimony of his friends and neighbors, McMillan did not assume the role of absentee landowner or gentrified overseer. Rather, he worked hard on his various groves and sweated alongside the laborers hired to plant, prune, harvest and care for the orange trees. Despite his success,

Modest settler's house. It is likely Sam McMillan's house resembled this one. *Sanford Museum Collection.*

Orange grove near Orlando, Florida. *Library of Congress.*

however, he was "penurious" and "close about spending" money on personal items or comforts and cautious all around in business affairs. Because of this, he got the reputation around town of being a miserly sort.

He wore shoes that he won in a bet with friend William Hawkins. He had one good coat and matching pants that he called his "visiting suit," but otherwise, he wore nondescript work clothes. He did his own cooking, didn't drink or smoke, slept on a cot and had little furniture or comforts inside his house.

Curiously, despite the Spartan living, he did own several thick gold rings, two or three gold pocket watches and "a large gold nugget he wanted to wear as a pin, just as they pick up out west" according to a friend. It seems that at one point earlier in life, he had traveled to "the Black Hills and got that and had that mounted."

He was not married when he arrived in Florida in 1874 and did not marry while building his land and citrus operation. He lived alone, which a few folks found peculiar for a man of his age (over forty-five). Known as Sam to most of his neighbors and Sammy to a few close ones, McMillan kept to himself but was described as "kind hearted," "affable," "quiet," "orderly" and "neighborly." Neighbor Charles Saint described his friend as follows:

> Q: Was he a social man?
> A: Well, yes, he was socially inclined, very much so.
>
> Q: Did he have many friends?
> A: Well, I don't know that he had many enemies. He was a man that was very much opposed to having enemies. He would do almost anything in the world to keep from having enemies, so much so that he did not register here for fear that would give him enemies.
>
> * * *
>
> Q: State how you know he didn't register for that cause?
> A: He told me that he did not want to register on account of probably its causing him to have enemies on one side or the other—that was the reason. I registered and tried to persuade him to register, and he gave me that reason for not registering.

Saint was talking about registering to vote in the 1876 presidential election. It was to be a referendum on the scandal-plagued administration of Ulysses Grant, post–Civil War Reconstruction and an economic slump gripping the nation. Sam apparently didn't want to take sides and was right to do so—the election turned out to be the most contentious and controversial in American history. Multiple ties in the Electoral College and accusations of fraudulent vote counting and registration resulted in the Compromise of 1877: Republican Rutherford B. Hayes was named president, and federal troops would withdraw from the South and formally end Reconstruction.

Politics aside, Sam McMillan mostly kept to himself; this latter trait may be attributable to a speech impediment. Over the years, Sam had lost every tooth in his upper jaw. He had a full set of upper false teeth, but these did not stay in place. In fact, they often slipped down and interfered with his ability to speak clearly. A close friend said that the teeth "were loose, they were a set that didn't fit very good, and in talking they would kind of slide down sometimes." Despite being a successful landowner and citrus grower, it seems that Sam couldn't get a set of false teeth that fit properly and may have been embarrassed to talk to people.

Downtown Sanford, Florida, circa 1886. *Chase Collection, University of Florida.*

Physically, in addition to the missing upper teeth, he had a ruddy complexion, a full beard, wasn't very tall and weighed approximately 125 to 130 pounds. Most importantly for our story, Sam McMillan had red hair: this would become the single most important fact in identifying his killer in a few short years.

THE NEIGHBORS

Desiring solitude, Sam McMillan intentionally chose the *middle* of his grove to build his modest house: it was barely visible through the trees and was half a mile to the nearest neighbor in any direction. Not surprisingly, he also craved security: when he left his house for anything other than daily work on his own land, he locked his gate with a strong metal hook and placed a heavy chain with a padlock around the posts. He then tied two pieces of wire around the gate slats so that he could tell if anyone had entered or tried to enter.

It's not clear where the paranoia stemmed from, since he lived among people he either knew from Ohio or was on friendly terms with. His immediate neighbors were a varied assortment of people who all knew

A neighboring house on Twin Lakes, Florida. *Sanford Museum Collection.*

Sam well and seemed used to his habits in a "that's just Sam" sort of way. They didn't interpret his peculiarities, solitude and security as directed toward them and accepted Sam as one of their own. They all would figure prominently in his murder trial.

J.O. Tabor was the closest neighbor who lived on the other side of Upper Twin Lake and perhaps knew Sam the best; he was from Salem, Ohio, knowing Sam since 1857. Tabor had moved to Florida in 1871 and seems to have been instrumental in convincing Sam to join the tide of Ohioans moving south, helping Sam get established when he arrived. Tabor owned his own orange grove, was the local postmaster and a onetime justice of the peace, and he played the role of elder statesman in the neighborhood.

In his testimony at Archie Newton's murder trial, Tabor described his friend Sam as follows:

> *Q: What were his habits and characteristics, to your knowledge?*
> *A: He was a very quiet, orderly man and a miserly turn, and lived by himself, a hardworking, honest man.*
>
> *Q: What were his habits regarding money?*
> *A: He loved money.*
>
> ** * **
>
> *Q: State whether or not he ever gave you any explanation of his habit of carrying his money with him?*
> *A: He did.*
>
> *Q: What was that?*
> *A: That he would trust no one here he knew to take care of it for him.*
>
> *Q: Was he or not on friendly, intimate terms with you?*
> *A: As much as any one, I think.*
>
> ** * **
>
> *Q: Was he by habit and character distrustful?*
> *A: I think so.*

Charles Saint lived next to Tabor and had been friends with Sam for about twelve years. He too was from Salem and had met and befriended Sam there. Saint appears to have been one of Sam's closest friends in Florida and sometimes visited Sam's house several times a day. Saint would later physically confront Archie Newton about the disappearance of his friend, whom he described as:

Q: State what his habits were, his character?
A: Well, he was rather a peculiar character. He lived by himself, kept back, lived alone all the time. He was alone when he was missed.

* * *

Q: Was he at all inclined to combativeness?
A: No sir, he was the most innocent man I ever seen. He was innocent as a baby.

Neighbor Leslie Miller was from, you guessed it, Salem, Ohio. Sam had known Miller's parents but didn't really befriend Leslie until he relocated to Florida in 1874. He apparently was very trustworthy, however, since he was the only person to occasionally live with Sam; according to Leslie, he worked for McMillan on and off over an eight-year period in McMillan's groves, often staying in Sam's house for months at a time.

His insight about Sam's habits and nature were similar to the others:

Q: State for the jury what McMillan's habits were—what sort of a man he was generally.
A: He was rather peculiar in his habits, not very liberal, but willing for everybody to have what was coming to them. He would pay up to the cent everytime he owed and had no disposition to cheat anybody out of anything, as far as I knew, he was a good honest man.

* * *

Q: What were his characteristics, as a man, was he frank and open, or distrustful and suspicious?
A: Rather the latter.

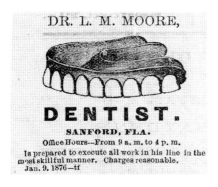

DR. L. M. MOORE,

DENTIST.

SANFORD, FLA.

Office Hours—From 9 a. m. to 4 p. m.
Is prepared to execute all work in his line in the most skillful manner. Charges reasonable.
Jan. 9. 1876—tf

Advertisement for Dr. Lindley Moore, local dentist and Sam McMillan's neighbor. *Sanford Museum Collection.*

Local dentist Lindley Moore lived directly to the east of Sam's grove, on Eureka Avenue. He too was from Ohio, hailing from the county adjacent to the one in which Sam had grown up. Moore was an outgoing Quaker and had the habit (which many found strange) of hanging about the Sanford docks and greeting all newcomers, a veritable one-man "Welcome to Sanford" committee. He was appointed justice of the peace in 1872 and wrote a personal letter of thanks to Henry Sanford for helping him get the job.

Interestingly, Dr. Moore grew to despise Henry Sanford and hated his politics; in December 1880, as Archie Newton began to settle in and look for property, Moore was denied a postmaster appointment and started a letter-writing campaign against Sanford. He also filed a civil lawsuit against Henry Sanford in 1880 (apparently for a breach of contract)—it was so acrimonious that Sanford actually filed a motion to change venue because he didn't think the court could be fair and impartial.

Downtown Sanford. *Sanford Museum Collection.*

THE WALLET

As we've seen from his friends and neighbors, Sam McMillan was generally suspicious of almost everyone. This led him to keep large amounts of cash on his person and at his house because he didn't trust banks to deposit his money in or people to hold it for him. Several friends recounted numerous conversations they had with McMillan over the years about the risk of keeping so much cash and not using a bank. Most thought it was foolish of him to do so—he was inviting trouble. His cash hoard was so well known in the community that some feared for his safety.

After he was arrested in October 1882, Archie Newton even blamed McMillan for keeping so much cash around: "McMillan ought to have been killed for carrying large sums of money about him in the way that he did, thereby tempting some one to take it from him in getting me into this trouble."

Most of the time, Sam carried his cash in a bulky wallet/passbook that fit either in an inner coat or vest pocket or inside a special pocket he sewed inside his shirts. It was described as "rather a rusty wallet, tied with a shoe string generally," and was so bulky that it was almost always visible no matter what pocket he put it in. The wallet may have been an almanac or a passbook, and Tabor thought it was "Stow's Almanac," which he had picked up at the post office and delivered to McMillan early in 1882. According to Tabor, McMillan liked having the almanac handy to refer to for information and to keep his money secure.

Whatever it was, Sam carried it everywhere with him, and several witnesses said that when he took it out of his inner pocket and untied it, a large "nest" of cash was visible. Several storekeepers would later comment that Sam often asked to come behind the counter or into a back room to take the wallet out, untie it and add or remove cash. Sanford storekeeper John Dodd said that the cash inside was significant and included many denominations of bills, including multiple hundreds.

Friends also commented that if Sam was going somewhere for longer than a day, he also brought a gold watch in a vest or coat pocket and two or three gold rings wrapped in buckskin that he kept in an inside pocket. He sometimes wore one of the thick gold rings to church, on special occasions or for visiting someone's house. And any valuables he left at home were secured "under lock and key" in two large trunks.

Charles Saint summed it up perfectly:

Q: State whether or not McMillan was a suspicious man?
A: I should think he was.

Q: Do you know?
A: Yes, I know he was.

"TIRED OF THIS LIFE"

By late 1881, Sam was tired of working in the salubrious climate of Florida and wanted to go back to Ohio. He asked a citrus dealer with whom he was friends, S.B. Harrington, to help him find a buyer for one of his smaller parcels (in Altamonte). Within a month, Harrington facilitated the sale of the land for $1,300. After closing, McMillan was paid the money "in greenbacks" at Dodd's general store in Sanford.

He then turned to selling his main grove at Twin Lakes.

There may have been another reason Sam wanted to sell his Florida land and return to Ohio. In August 1882, about six weeks before his disappearance, Sam told one of his laborers—A. Pichard—that he was "tired of this life" and was going to sell everything. He then showed Pichard a picture of a woman and a letter she had written. Pichard was French, and English was his second language. It's therefore interesting that he commented about the handwriting being very nice and said, "I see she is writing good English." Sam didn't give any more details about the mystery woman, but he didn't disagree when Pichard said that he'd no longer be a bachelor after he returned to Ohio.

This is tantalizing information, but Pichard didn't elaborate further on the identity of the woman, whether she was foreign-born or whether McMillan was engaged or intended to return to Ohio to marry her.

By this time, Archie and Kate Newton were settled in their new home about a mile or so from Sam's property, a short horse ride away. Archie was busy working on his orange trees (also using the services of the Frenchman A. Pichard for labor) and seemed to be on his way to a gentrified respectability that he and Kate probably craved (especially Kate). But it seems he was already thinking about more and wanted to expand his holdings. The entire Twin Lakes area knew that Sam wanted to sell his land and return to Ohio, and he had already discussed pricing with several people. That's when Archie cast his eyes on Sam's land.

Harvesting oranges in the 1880s. *Sanford Museum Collection.*

We don't know when Archie first talked to Sam about buying his large orange grove, but it appears to have occurred sometime in 1882, possibly as early as February. The neighborhood generally knew that McMillan was asking a hefty price for the parcel, which wasn't surprising since it was now producing an extensive crop every year. Archie would have known this information as well and certainly would have made a more detailed inquiry. But in the course of talking to Sam, Archie also seemed very curious about how much money Sam actually had in his possession. In dramatic testimony at the murder trial, Leslie Miller gave the following account of conversations he had with Newton several months before Sam's murder, which the prosecutor used to establish motive:

> *Q: Have you ever had any conversations with him about Samuel McMillan before McMillan's disappearance?*
> *A: Yes sir.*
>
> *Q: Just state as near as you can recollect, what the conversation was.*
> *A: He asked me in regard to selling Mr. McMillan's grove for him.*

Q: Go on.
A: As to whether [I] *could act as agent for him. I told him I thought not, and that if the grove was sold he would be apt to sell it himself. He inquired as to what kind of a man he was, living as he didn't need to live that way, if he didn't have plenty of money.*

Q: When you say that, do you mean Newton asked you if McMillan had plenty of money?
A: Yes sir.

Q: Now go on with the conversation.
A: I told him I did not know how much he was worth, he had told me that his own brothers did not know how much money he was worth. McMillan said that.

Q: In that conversation, did or not Mr. Newton ask you any questions concerning McMillan's habit of living?

Objected to by defense.
Overruled. Exception taken.

A: Yes sir.

Q: What was it?
A: Well he thought it wasn't necessary for him to live that way, fixed as he was, thought he was peculiar.

Q: Was anything said by Mr. Newton in that conversation touching McMillan's carrying any money about with him?

Objected to by defense.
Overruled. Exception taken.

A: Yes sir.

Q: What did he say?
A: Wanted to know if he didn't carry his money with him, asked if he wasn't too miserly to deposit it in a bank or trust any body with it. He also asked how much I thought he carried with him. Wanted me to state

how much, told him I couldn't tell him. He thought probably about fifteen thousand or twenty thousand dollars. I told him I had no idea that he carried that much with him.

Q: Let me understand now distinctly—was it Newton that said to you he thought McMillan carried fifteen or twenty thousand dollars with him? A: He asked me if I didn't think he did just the same thing.

Q: Point out to the jury which Newton it was that as this conversation with you.

Witness points to the accused.

This conversation, aside from the courtroom drama it provided, tells us several important things. First, Newton knew McMillan fairly well by early 1882 and knew that he wanted to sell his land. It doesn't seem that the Newtons were close friends of Sam, and as we've seen, Sam was fairly distrustful of those he didn't know and slow to open up. It's also apparent that in the political atmosphere of the Florida frontier, there was a general distrust of foreigners. Archie and Kate were not Americans, would have spoken with a pronounced British accent and had the benefit of wealthy (foreign) benefactors who bought the land, the house and the grove for them. Every one in town would have known this.

Second, Archie seems to have been pretty serious about making a bid to buy McMillan's land. This indicates that he intended to stay and settle on the Florida frontier or at least establish himself there. It also shows that he either felt good about his skills and prospects as a citrus producer (even though he had just started) or that he was trying to play the role of wealthy gentry like his uncle and great-uncle. It's also possible that he was just obsessed with money and desperately wanted to be successful for himself and Kate.

Third and most notably, Archie must have thought that he could get his hands on a significant amount of cash. Sam had made it known, in several "private" conversations, that his asking price for the fifteen-acre parcel, the house and the profitable grove was about $16,000. This equates to approximately $395,000 in 2018 dollars.

Central Florida land sales at this time were moderate to strong. Sam's expectations were on the high side but were not unreasonable. A special supplement to the *South Florida Journal* issued on September

Orange picking on the Florida frontier. *Sanford Museum Collection.*

20, 1882, included information about land sales from Richard H. Marks and the Orange County Land Agency. The data reportedly showed robust sales and strong prices in and around Sanford and Orlando.

A few months later, on April 5, 1883, the *Sanford Journal* reported, "On a brief visit to our county seat on Monday last, we found the boom of progress unabated. The cry is 'still they come!'"

In this land boom, Archie and Kate must have thought they could come up with $15,000 to $16,000 in cash (Sam would not accept a draft or bank check) in early to mid-1882. Given the fact that Archie was living on $83 a month (Ingraham's view was that Archie spent every penny and needed the allowance each month) and considering that he had to ask for special allowances throughout 1881 and 1882 for tools, furniture, hardware, additional citrus products and so on, it's not likely he had saved anywhere near this amount by 1882.

And given the fact that Kate Newton had been essentially destitute during her time in London and back at Hull, and the fact that her mother had closed down the London boardinghouse for lack of funds, it's not likely she had this amount of money stashed away.

The only logical conclusion here is that Archie had either asked his uncle for the money or had some expectation that he could get it from the Florida Land and Colonization Company, Uncle Gray or Sir William MacKinnon himself. It was indeed a hefty sum for the young couple, one that just a year or so before they wouldn't have dared dream about.

Whatever the case, Newton talked openly with several people during the spring and summer of 1882 about buying Sam's land.

He told his friend Andrew Middlemas that Kate had "taken a fancy" to Sam's grove, he would buy it with her money and it would be hers. He also noted that Sam was asking the "extravagant" price of $16,000.

He later told another friend, Emile Tissot, about his desire to purchase McMillan's place: "I will [buy it] if he comes down to my figure." Newton said that he wanted to pay $13,000. This was still an enormous sum given the Newtons' financial situation.

Despite Archie's talk around town and the confidence he must have projected about having money to spend, Sam didn't care much for him. He didn't think the twenty-one-year-old Englishman was serious about being able to buy his land and didn't initially engage in any serious discussions.

But his opinion changed after Newton formally visited and inspected the grove in August 1882 in the company of another Englishman, William Beardall.

Beardall also worked for the Florida Land and Colonization Company. He was a personal confidant of Archie's Uncle Gray, and Gray used him for back channel investigations and reporting. Beardall had been sent to Florida to check on the company's holdings and report directly back to the board, which by this time did not trust Henry Sanford's assessments of value, prospects and so on. In this way, Beardall was used to bypass Sanford, check on Ingraham's work and correspond with no one but Gray.

Sam evidently knew of Beardall's role on behalf of the company and was impressed by this Englishman: "That young man is one of the first employees of General Sanford's agents, and I suppose he will not come here and talk about business unless it would be done."

After the inspection, serious negotiations ensued between Sam and Archie.

Around this time, Tabor had several discussions with Sam about the potential sale and negotiations with Archie, negotiations Tabor called "no secret" in the neighborhood. Sam was upset that people knew about and were discussing his negotiations with Archie, because from the sale, he would receive a large amount of money—or possibly gold—and he didn't like anyone knowing that. He also indicated that Archie had agreed to keep the negotiations private.

According to Tabor, Archie formally offered Sam $13,500 for the land and grove. In separate conversations, Archie asked Tabor what he thought about that price. Tabor demurred, not wishing to talk about his neighbors. But he pointed out that an adjoining property (O.O. Smith) had recently sold for $10,000 and suggested it may have been the more valuable of the two. He told Newton that further research should be done regarding other prices in the area.

Tabor also asked Sam how Newton intended to pay for the land. Sam responded that Newton had said in so many words that he had this amount of money "in gold" stored at his house. Tabor was incredulous:

I told him that if Mr. Newton made such a statement, he was an idiot or a knave, that no sane man would make any such statement. While I didn't know anything about Mr. Newton's circumstances, he might have that money. I didn't believe he had that money in that shape in the lone house.

McMillan had also told the laborer Pichard of Archie's claims of having so much money at his house, saying a few weeks before his disappearance: "If he was wanting to buy my grove, he would not make it so public, and he will not make the people suppose he has so much money to pay for it because some robber [might] come and rob him."

Since there were questions about the Newtons' ability to pay, Tabor suggested that any sale of McMillan's land should be done through a New York bank to transfer and guarantee money. He also told Sam to inquire of James Ingraham to confirm that Newton had access to such sums, whether cash or gold. It was even suggested that Archie had this gold locked up with Ingraham in Sanford, although this seems unlikely and there are no records of such arrangement.

By September 15, 1882, things had progressed such that Newton invited Sam over for tea so they could complete a deal. Sam asked Tabor if he should accept this invitation and go to the Newton home; Tabor said that he "most certainly" should, especially if a favorable deal could be reached and Newton could pay.

But in his preparations to sell that summer, Sam had discovered that his deed didn't accurately describe his parcel and needed to be corrected. By the time of Newton's invitation, McMillan hadn't yet taken any steps to have this done. Sam feared this would impede the sale and told Newton about it.

Archie told him to come anyway. Kate also insisted; she wanted Sam to give them the title, receive the money and be done. Title corrections could be done afterward.

Sam accepted the fateful invitation. At dusk on September 30, right around 6:00 p.m., Newton and McMillan were seen walking together along the pathway that led from McMillan's and Tabor's properties to the Newton home.

It was the last time anyone saw Sam McMillan alive.

5
DISAPPEARANCE

SATURDAY, SEPTEMBER 30

Heading to Tea

What exactly happened to Sam McMillan remains a mystery to this day.

Hired hand Richard Cooper said he worked for Sam on Thursday, September 28, until about noon. That's when the "fertilizer gave out" and they had to stop for the day. Sam told Cooper he would get more fertilizer and instructed him to come back the following Tuesday to finish.

Another local, Zeri Adams, claimed to have talked to Archie on Friday between 2:00 and 3:00 p.m. and asked about the purchase of Sam's land. Newton told Adams that he had "bought the grove" and was "going to New York the first of the week to see about the money he had there to pay for it." Strangely, he told Adams that he did not know the exact amount of money he actually had or "the shape it was in" but would clear all that up when he went to New York the following week.

He also told Adams that he felt that he would have enough money to buy Sam's grove, invest in a proposed new railroad line in the area (Archie would "put up a mile" in the line) and, if he had enough money left over, buy some stock in a venture that Adams had floated as a possibility. Is this evidence that Archie had received or thought he would receive a large sum of money from his uncle or MacKinnon?

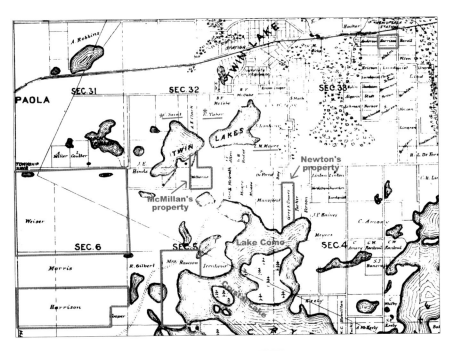

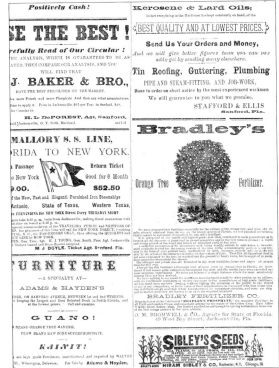

Above: Detailed map of area of Sam McMillan's disappearance. *Sanford Museum Collection.*

Left: Advertisement for the most important element of orange growing. *Sanford Museum Collection.*

Charles Saint last saw Sam on Friday evening about sundown. They had been conversing at Sam's place; Saint asked if there was anything new regarding the sale of the land to Newton, and Sam said that it "remained the same." Sam did not mention that he was going to leave home that weekend or embark on any sort of trip outside of the county or state. He also mentioned to Saint that he had been sick the past few days and wasn't feeling well.

Tabor saw Sam on Saturday afternoon, September 30, when Sam stopped by for a brief visit. Their conversation was cursory, and Sam did not talk of taking a trip or leaving that weekend.

After visiting Tabor's place, we know that Sam went home, got cleaned up and dressed in some of his nicer clothes. He left for Newton's around sundown, walking east down Eureka Avenue and turning off onto the footpath toward Lake Como.

How are we certain of this? Because there was an eyewitness: Mrs. Francis Stewart. Actually, she was eyewitness to several key events, which she described in riveting testimony at trial:

Q: Did you know Mr. Samuel McMillan in his lifetime?
A: Yes sir.

Q: When did you last see Mr. Samuel McMillan alive?
A: On a Saturday eve.

Q: Can you remember what Saturday eve it was?
A: No sir.

Q: How long after you last saw him did you hear of his being missing?
A: The next week.

Q: About what time on this Saturday evening was it that you saw him?
A: Just after sundown.

Q: Was he alone, or was anybody with him?
A: Mr. Newton was with him.
Q: What Mr. Newton?
A: Mr. A. W. Newton.

Q: If he is present in the courtroom, point him out to the jury.
Witness points out the accused to the jury.

Q: Were they walking together, or driving, or what?
A: They were walking.

Q: In what direction were they going?
A: They were going by the side of the lake.

Q: In what way were they going?
Witness says she does not understand the question.

Q: What lake were they going by the side of?
A: Christal Lake.

Q: Did you know where Mr. Newton's place is?
A: Yes sir.

Q: Now state whether or not they were going in the direction of Mr. Newton's place.
A: Yes sir.

Q: Did you see Mr. Newton's wife that eve?
A: Yes sir.

Q: Where did you see her?
A: I saw her going toward Mr. Harrison's store.

Q: Did you see her when she came back?
A: Yes sir.

Q: Which way did she go?
A: She was going towards the house.

Q: Whose house?
A: Mr. Newton's.

Q: Was she driving or walking?
A: She was driving.

Q: Tell the jury how you saw them, where they were and everything you know about it in your own way.
A: I first saw Mrs. Newton going towards Mr. Harrison's store in the buggy alone, and in about ½ an hour after Mr. Newton came along walking, and when she came back ½ an hour afterwards Mr. Newton and Mr. McMillan came along walking and they walked down by the side of the lake going towards Mr. Newton's house. That is all I know about it.

This excerpt gives us confirmation of several key facts. (It also reminds us that witnesses aren't always clear, and the lawyers questioning them don't always establish the clarity we'd like when reading 130 years later.)

Mrs. Stewart had briefly been staying at a house she identified as "Mrs. Clark's" when she saw Sam, Archie and Kate on Saturday, September 30, 1882. Unfortunately, she wasn't asked to specifically describe where the house was located, probably because everyone knew whose house it was and where it was situated.

There is a property owned by "A.K. Clark" indicated on the map of Twin Lakes, but it is on the northern side of the lakes. Mrs. Stewart testified that Eureka Avenue was to the south, about 150 yards away, and the Newtons' house was to the east. The Clark house faced east–west, and she saw the comings and goings while she was standing in the doorway. These indicators suggest that the A.K. Clark house on Twin Lake could have been where Stewart was standing when she saw Newton and McMillan.

Although she was a little confused about the road names, she was clear that Kate Newton had driven by in the buggy on the "main road" (Eureka Avenue) in the direction of Mr. Harrison's store (heading west). Thirty minutes later, she saw Archie walk along the same road toward McMillan's grove (also heading west). She wouldn't have been able to see Sam's house from there, since it was in the middle of his grove and not by the street or on the lake. She therefore wouldn't have seen Newton traverse Sam's gate or at the front door.

Thirty minutes after that, Mrs. Stewart saw Kate drive back by on Eureka Avenue toward her own house (heading east), and Archie and Sam soon followed on foot, proceeding a little ways down Eureka Avenue and then turning off down the footpath that led along Crystal Lake, Lake Como and to Newton's house.

The facts of Mrs. Stewart's story are partially confirmed by Zeri Adams.

Earlier on Saturday, September 30, McMillan had given Adams some money and a grocery list since Adams was riding into town and would pick up a few things. The list included granulated sugar, a "barrel of bones" (the fertilizer that Sam needed to continue working with), oatmeal and a bottle of Simmons Liver Regulator.

Adams spent the entire day in Sanford, however, drinking "beer and other things." He didn't arrive back at McMillan's until between 8:00 and 9:00 p.m. on Saturday night with the groceries. But Sam was not home. Unsure what to do and probably inebriated, Adams left the barrel in the grove and the groceries on a chair "in the porch between the two houses" in the hopes that McMillan would see them when he got home.

The statements of Mrs. Stewart and Zeri Adams confirm that Sam accepted the invitation for tea and pinpoint his departure with Archie around 6:00 p.m. They also establish that Sam still wasn't home by 9:00 p.m.

When he left with Archie at 6:00 p.m. that Saturday evening, Sam must have expected to have some fine English tea with Archie and Kate, discuss the issues with his deed and perhaps come to an agreement on price and payment. He probably wasn't clear if the Newtons had $15,000 in cash or maybe gold at their house, and there is no record that he ever inquired with Ingraham or any banks in Sanford about Archie's ability to pay. And from Archie's own comments to Zeri Adams the day before, even he didn't know how much money he had.

SUNDAY, OCTOBER 1

Looking for a Sharp Razor

None of Sam's neighbors saw him after Saturday afternoon, September 30. In fact, no one in this tight-knit community saw him walking on the road, working in his grove, riding to church or shopping at the store. His two closest friends, Tabor and Saint, did not recall seeing or speaking with him on Sunday, October 1 or in the days following. This was a little off routine, but wasn't entirely unusual, especially given Sam's penchant for privacy.

But neighbors *did* see Archie Newton on Sunday, starting quite early in the day.

As recounted by several neighbors and friends, his behavior that day was a collection of strange activities and odd statements.

He showed up to the house of laborer A. Pichard around 8:00 a.m. According to Mrs. Mercy Pichard, Newton "said that he come to talk business with Mr. Pichard." She told him that her husband had left to go get milk at a neighbor's, but to come in and wait. Archie accepted and asked for a bottle of wine while he waited because he didn't feel well and hadn't slept well the night before.

Mercy gave him a "small" bottle of wine while they waited. This apparently was not an unusual request because Newton had bought wine from her before. As an interesting side note, Mercy also was English.

Mr. Pichard returned, and the men talked about how much Archie owed for Pichard's hours of labor in Archie's orange grove over the past few weeks. Pichard told him it was about thirty dollars total, the same amount Pichard had asked to be paid just two days earlier. Archie had promised to pay Pichard after going to town and getting the money "next week."

We must here expand on Pichard's colorful background, which belied his current work as an orange grove laborer. At fifty-seven years old, Pichard was a robust hardworking man whose wife just had a baby a few months before. He was French and spoke English with a heavy accent. He had lived in Paris, Marseilles, Algiers, New Orleans, New York and Florida. He was commissioned as a doctor by the emperor of Brazil while he resided in Paris but had no medical training and had never been to Brazil; instead, he obtained this designation via mail. He first arrived in Florida at Tallahassee, then moved to Jacksonville with the great migration of African Americans for the 1876 election and then relocated to Sanford for work, where he intersected with McMillan and Newton.

Archie finished his conversation with Pichard and then rode to Zeri Adams's house, which stood on the same road and less than a few minutes away. Adams had just left his house on horseback around 9:00 or 9:30 a.m. to head to McMillan's and make sure Sam got the groceries he had left at his house the night before and encountered Newton on the road. Newton asked if Adams had a "sharp razor" he could borrow. Archie explained that he and Kate were expecting company that evening and he wanted a clean shave. Adams went back to his house and loaned him a razor, and noted that Newton used it to shave. But it's not clear from the court records whether he did this at Adams's house (which would be odd) or if he took the razor with him to use later.

They talked for a bit, and as he departed, Newton inquired again about the "stock company" that Adams earlier indicated he was starting. Archie said he "now had some money" to invest. But Adams told Newton that the idea had fallen apart and that he had made other arrangements on the business front.

They parted without another word, although Adams had decided not to ride to McMillan's place after all because it was raining.

Archie next rode to his friend Emile Tissot's house, arriving sometime between 9:00 and 10:00 a.m. Tissot lived a little farther west toward the town of Paola and was surprised to see his friend that Sunday morning. He said that Archie intended to borrow a razor but explained that he had already stopped by Zeri Adams's house and borrowed his. In the course of their conversation, Newton asked if Tissot knew whether Adams had bought the *Sanford Journal,* as had been rumored about town; Tissot did not know. Tissot asked if Newton knew that Harry True had returned to town the day before—Newton had not known and asked Tissot to go to True's with him. Tissot declined.

Zeri Adams, who strangely loaned Archie a sharp razor the morning after McMillan's disappearance. *Sanford Museum Collection.*

Archie then showed up at the home of Fred True, about a mile from Tissot's. Fred, his brother Harry and another local, William Hawkins, were there as well. Harry True had "just come back from the coast," and the men sat down to talk about his trip and local gossip. It is evident from the recollections of this visit that Newton was on pretty friendly terms with these men, especially since a few sat in chairs and Harry lounged on the bed.

Fred True noted the bottle of wine in Archie's pocket, and Archie explained that it was "for his wife." He then told the group that he had fired a shot at an alligator at his house the night before. He used the Colt double-action .38 pistol he had borrowed a few weeks before from Fred. Fred said that Newton had asked to borrow the gun to "protect himself or some such reason as that." Kate would later tell Fred that they slept with the gun under their pillow at night ostensibly for security. The men must have been incredulous at Archie's recounting that he had fired the gun at an alligator (the night before, no less), since Archie was not the rough-and-tumble type to handle a gun and shoot at alligators in the dark.

Archie would soon regret telling this story, however, as the gun and its firing would be key pieces of evidence against him.

Later that Sunday, between 5:00 and 6:00 p.m., Archie and Kate showed up at the home of Kettie Munson in Sanford. She wasn't expecting them, but they were good friends and she was not troubled by their arrival. But this was more than a social call—the Newtons asked to stay with the Munsons and ended up staying almost two weeks. Newton later paid Mrs. Munson fifteen dollars for the stay.

When the Newtons arrived, Mrs. Munson noticed that Kate's dress was quite soiled, especially along the bottom. She asked what happened, and Kate explained that it got dirty the night before when she went to get the horse while her husband went "down to the lake." Kate said this occurred *after* McMillan had left their house.

MONDAY, OCTOBER 2

The Prized Lemonade Pitcher

Pichard had worked most of the preceding month for Archie Newton at $1.75 per day and was scheduled to keep working in October. On Monday, October 2, he dutifully showed up a little after 7:00 a.m. for work. He wasn't aware that the Newtons had spent Sunday night at the Munson house in Sanford and were not home; he assumed they were still asleep inside the house. So he elected not to knock on the door and instead commenced work in the "northern section" of Newton's grove, planting and tending to trees, moving west to east as he worked.

On his way to Newton's that morning, Pichard had cut through the edge of McMillan's grove (as he often did) and made a cut of some citron buds as Newton had requested. He was going to ask Sam for permission, but he wasn't there and Pichard assumed it would be alright since Sam and Archie knew each other.

He noticed that Sam's gate was shut but not double padlocked, and there was no smoke from the chimney. Pichard said that he saw some of Sam's tools stacked neatly in the porch area between the house and barn and a stack of rags used to cover the trees. The groceries that Zeri Adams had left on Saturday night were not there, but the barrel of fertilizer was in the grove.

Of particular import, Pichard noticed that one of Sam's most prized possessions—a pitcher from his dear aunt—was left outside on a tin wash basin. This pitcher was so important to Sam that he "would prefer to lose a hundred dollars than to break the pitcher." Pichard had used it several times before for lemonade and had been warned each time about how prized it was and how careful he needed to be. He therefore thought it very unusual that Sam would leave this pitcher outside overnight.

Hired hand Richard Cooper said that he did not hear from Sam on Monday as he expected to and therefore did not go to McMillan's grove to resume the fertilizer work.

MONDAY, OCTOBER 2

"Is that Sammy's Hoe Working in the Grove?"

Newton, who had spent Sunday night at the Munsons' in Sanford, arrived back at his own house around 11:00 a.m. on Monday in a buggy, accompanied by Mrs. Munson's adult son Eugene.

They conversed briefly with Pichard who was hard at work in the orange grove and then went into the house, where Archie went upstairs and changed into clean clothes. Munson said that he was in the room part of this time and saw Archie place a large "roll" of greenbacks onto the bed. Actually, according to Munson, Archie called his attention to it, although Munson was unclear as to why or exactly how. It turns out Archie had been quite busy earlier that morning with that roll of money.

He had stopped by the New York Clothing Store in Sanford first thing in the morning. The proprietor was S.L. Travis, who had befriended Archie when he first arrived in town. According to Travis, Archie bought $60 to $70 worth of clothes and other goods that Monday morning for himself and for the Munson family, including "Little Freddie Munson." He also wanted to pay off his account at the store, which was another $30 or so. Archie took a roll of cash from his pocket and counted out $10 bills to pay his account. Travis said that this was unusual of Newton, since he had never paid cash before, settled his bill in arrears "whenever it suited him" and usually paid with a bank check.

Eugene Munson worked at the New York Clothing Store and was scheduled for that Monday. While he was shopping, Archie asked Travis to let Eugene have the day off so he could accompany Newton about. Travis agreed.

Henry DeForest's store in downtown Sanford. *Sanford Museum Collection.*

Archie also ran into grocer C.H. Leffler that morning while in Sanford and settled another debt. Leffler watched Archie remove a large amount of bills from his pocket and count out fourteen five-dollar bills. According to Leffler, the bills were smooth but not brand new: "They had the appearance of bills that had been selected, smoothed out and put away, and at laid at full length they were all well-preserved bills." This was similar to the way Sam stored his money in the passbook/wallet and drew an intriguing inference about their origin.

After Archie changed clothes at his house with Eugene Munson in attendance, the two men rode out in the buggy and turned left on Eureka Avenue on their way to Paola. As they approached McMillan's property just down the road, Archie remarked that he figured they would see McMillan working in the grove as usual. As they passed by the grove and talked about the orange trees looking very fine, Archie pointedly asked, "Is that Sammy's hoe working in the grove?" He said it was glistening in the sun and implored of Eugene: "Don't you see it?"

But Eugene saw nothing and, under withering questioning later on at the murder trial, maintained that he never saw a glint of metal in McMillan's grove as he drove by on that Monday with Archie.

Hardware store owned by J. Hill, where Archie Newton bought many of his supplies. *Sanford Museum Collection.*

They rode on to Harrison's store in Paola, where Archie produced the roll of cash again and paid off his account there ($56.00). They went from Harrison's store to the home of J.H. Woodson and then stopped at another general goods store to buy more wine.

After finishing his work for Archie later that day, Pichard stopped back at Sam's house on Monday evening on his way home to ask for a container of varnish that Archie said he had "forgotten" at McMillan's. But neither McMillan nor the varnish was there.

Later on Monday evening, Archie rode back out to Pichard's house and paid him the thirty dollars he owed and they had discussed on Archie's early-morning visit the day before. According to Pichard's recollection, he was paid in a combination of bills and silver.

WEDNESDAY, OCTOBER 4

Brand-New Furniture

Two more days passed before Zeri Adams ran into Archie while in Sanford on Wednesday, and they talked about Sam. No one had seen him since Saturday. Zeri was perplexed, but Archie felt that Sam was probably in Deland (a town north of Sanford), visiting his property there, and would be back soon.

While working on Wednesday, Pichard says that Newton told him that he (Newton) had seen McMillan on Monday working in his grove as he drove past with Eugene Munson. Archie said they saw the "light of his hoe" in the grove. They had this conversation as Newton was getting his bags to go to Jacksonville or "somewhere north."

Another day laborer named Prince McFadden went to Archie's house on Wednesday—not to work, but to go fishing. When he arrived with his two children, no one was home. Since he had standing permission from the Newtons to use their boat and their dock, he took Newton's boat and went fishing. He later commented that the boat appeared to have been recently cleaned.

When Pichard stopped by McMillan's on Wednesday after work and he still wasn't there, he went to Tabor's house to report it. Tabor thought McMillan "had gone to Volusia" and said not to worry about him, but Pichard was very uneasy and thought Sam may have been sick. Tabor's wife convinced him to go have a look because Pichard was so uneasy. Using lanterns as it grew dusk, they went to McMillan's grove to investigate, but it was too dark to see anything.

Pichard suggested that they get Charles Saint to join them the following morning "because in France, the law requires three men to go into an empty house." When the trio peered into the windows of Sam's on Thursday morning, they didn't see anything amiss. The exterior was still the same, the tools still lined up in the porch area, the barrel of fertilizer still in the grove. They elected not to go inside, evidently thinking Sam was away on business.

After this brief look inside the windows, Pichard headed on to Newton's to work. Around 11:00 a.m., a wagon with brand-new furniture arrived (driven by "Little Munson"), followed by the Newtons in a brand-new buggy. It seemed that Archie was still on a spending spree with his unusually large roll of cash, something the entire neighborhood now noticed.

Part of the waterfront at Sanford, Florida, 1882. *Sanford Museum Collection.*

Pichard held the gate for the procession and later mentioned that he had not seen Sam in a few days. Newton replied, "What's all the fuss about McMillan—he's in Volusia."

Throughout the rest of that week and into the next, however, Sam neither returned to Twin Lakes nor was heard from. Suggestion that he was at Deland or another property turned to curiosity as to his whereabouts. Friends and neighbors began asking about, wondering where Sam was and if he was alright. As the days passed, their curiosity turned to concern and then to fear that something bad had happened to him.

By October 10, the people of Twin Lakes began to talk of foul play. J.O. Tabor took out the following notice in the paper:

Information Wanted
Sanford, FL Oct. 10, 1882

Editor Journal:

Much anxiety is felt by the citizens of this vicinity (Twin Lakes) regarding the disappearance of Mr. Samuel McMillan, who owns a grove here. If any person has seen or heard of him since 3 o'clock p.m. Saturday, they will confer a favor by communication with the undersigned.

Florida Agriculturist, Orange County Reporter, *and* Tavares Herald *please copy on insertion and send bill to*

J.O. Tabor, Sanford, FL

Kate Newton saw Dr. Lindley Moore on October 11 and told him that Sam had come to their house for tea on the night of Saturday, September 30, and walked home by himself around 9:00 p.m. This seems to be the first time the Newtons confirmed that Sam had in fact come to their home on Saturday evening and probably did nothing to quell the rumors that were starting to circulate.

Dr. Moore also said he spoke with Archie in Sanford on October 12 when he encountered him and Kate on the streets of Sanford:

> *I saw A.W. Newton in the town of Sanford between 9 and 10 o'clock in the street. He and his wife were together in a buggy; he first asked me quite a number of questions about the loss of McMillan, I answered them, and then I asked him if he had purchased Mr. McMillan's grove, as I heard reported? He replied: "No sir, I have not." and said "I have heard a great many reports too." and laughed at the same time, and then he drove off, that is, Newton. And at same time remarked: "I think it is very singular what became of McMillan."*

Moore wasn't asked what he thought about Newton's comments, but they do seem rather odd. And it isn't difficult to see how this exchange can be interpreted as sinister, the laugh maniacal even. Everyone now knew that Sam McMillan had visited the Newtons on the evening of Saturday, September 30, and hadn't been seen since.

Whispers soon followed the English couple everywhere they went.

6
SEARCHING FOR SAM

FIRST SEARCH, OCTOBER 13

The Coon Trap

On October 12, 1882, a local paper (*South Florida Journal*) noted that "there seems to be some mystery" connected with the disappearance of McMillan, and "it is feared that there has been foul dealings with him."

The first formal search party met on the morning of October 13. Organized by local store owner and justice of the peace Edgar Harrison and attorney Thomas Wilson, a group of about ten men formed a line and fanned out in a circular pattern from McMillan's house. Archie Newton was among the searchers. Those on horseback scoured the brush, and a group went on foot to Newton's house, as Archie had agreed to use his rowboat to search the lake.

Tony Fox was in a group walking with Newton to Newton's house. Fox said that a water telescoper would be helpful to search the lake and asked if Archie would get one made for them to use. This device consisted of a long metal tube or cone-shaped vessel with a piece of thick glass at the end. It could be partially submerged below the water line to view under the surface or to the bottom of a body of water. According to Fox, Archie agreed that such a device would be helpful for searching the lake, but he didn't agree that he should be the one to order and pay for it.

But he must have thought more about it, since Archie actually did request a telescoper device to be made. In the next day or two, he went to the store of M.L. Holland in Sanford and asked Holland to make a cone-shaped vessel for him with glass at one end. He specifically told Holland that it was to be used in the search for McMillan's body, which by this time was the talk of the town. Holland later testified that he made the device and gave it to Archie the next day. The roll of cash undoubtedly came out once again to pay for it.

Archie volunteered his own rowboat and accompanied the group searching Lake Como on October 13. They spent a few hours carefully rowing along the northern portion of the lake, looking for any sign of McMillan's body or any clues as to his disappearance. Newton commented that the search was "a wild goose chase," and he was characterized as the "least enthusiastic" of the search party.

At one point, they spotted something floating in the water and quickly rowed to it. Edgar Harrison said that Archie stopped rowing, stood in the boat and stared at the object as they glided in close. It turned out to be an "upside down bonnet," and the group moved on.

Later in the morning, a member of the party searching on land named George Edwards discovered a pile of brush covering a heap of old fence rails or slats. The brush consisted of oak branches and appeared to have been recently lain. Edwards thought something or someone might be buried there but wanted others present when he moved everything.

He quickly rode to the lakeshore and called to the party on Newton's boat. He described what he had located and asked Archie if anyone was buried there since this appeared to be on his land. Archie said that a man who had drowned in the lake a few years ago had been buried in that area. He then asked Edwards if the spot was covered with old fence rails and brush. When Edwards answered in the affirmative, Newton replied, "Oh! that is a place I made for a coon trap."

They all went back to the spot. Underneath was what Edwards described as "a hole in appearance, like a grave." It was five and a half feet long, twenty inches wide and about two feet deep. The perfect size for burying a human body.

But the hole was empty.

ACCUSATIONS IN THE PARLOR

Later in the day, after the discovery of the "coon trap" and after they had stopped searching the lake, several men sat Archie down in the parlor of his house and discussed Sam's disappearance. Their efforts had turned up nothing that day, and the men were frustrated. Their session quickly denigrated into accusations and harsh questioning.

Archie confirmed to the men gathered around him in his parlor that Sam had indeed come over for tea on Saturday evening, around 6:00 p.m. Nervous in the face of this posse, Archie initially said they rode over together on horseback. He then said they rode in the buggy with Kate, but later changed that to say they walked. He said they drank coffee while they talked but then changed that to "tea" and nothing stronger. Archie didn't think Sam drank anything stronger anyway.

Tony Fox asked Newton what time Sam had left his place on Saturday night. Archie said 9:00 p.m. and never wavered on that time. He added that he and Kate stayed up until 1:00 or 2:00 playing cards, then went to bed.

Charles Saint asked if Newton heard any gunshots that night. Newton said no, but "if he had, he wouldn't have paid any attention to it because there were so many negroes shooting around the negro cabins." Interestingly, Archie did not tell the men that he had fired a shot at an alligator that night with a gun borrowed from Fred True.

The questions grew intense and then repetitive. Since it was approaching dinnertime (reportedly, Pichard had brought food and was sitting outside eating), the meeting broke up and the men wandered out. They all agreed to meet at another's house for dinner and discuss organizing a further search. Perhaps because he felt threatened by the group, or because he wanted to avoid further suspicion as Sam's disappearance seemingly shifted toward he and Kate, Archie agreed to attend.

But Charles Saint wasn't satisfied with Archie's story and wanted to conduct his own interrogation. He followed Archie onto the porch, and as they watched the others trudge or ride up the long driveway, he suddenly yanked the sleeve of Archie's coat and hit the younger man's leg with the stick he was carrying. We can imagine his snarl as he forcefully asked again where Sam had gone. Archie didn't retaliate or fight back but instead fumbled the same story about Sam coming around 6:00 p.m. and leaving around 9:00 p.m. on Saturday night, September 30. Saint then pointed down the driveway and asked which way Sam had gone when he left. As a wagonload of men proceeded away toward Eureka Avenue, Archie led Saint about seventy-five feet down the drive. He stopped, pointed and told Saint that this was where Sam had turned off the night he left and headed home. It was the path that ran diagonally to Sam's place.

Saint stood at the path turn off and barraged Archie with more questions about Sam's visit and departure. Perhaps to further explain himself, Archie got his own horse and rode with Saint along the shortcut to meet the others for dinner. On the way, Archie recovered and gave further explanation, apparently trying to rehabilitate himself in Saint's accusing eyes.

This included, quite curiously, his belief that Sam had been "hit in the head with a lightwood knot" and was somewhere in the lake. He asked Saint whether a man who was "hit in the head with a lightwood knot would bleed very much." Archie also spoke about the "negroes" living in the area, and seemed to suggest that perhaps they had something to do with Sam's disappearance.

They rode on and a few minutes later, Archie changed his opinion about the manner of death and said he bet that if McMillan's body were found, it would be discovered that he was shot by his (Newton's) gun. Archie seemed to suggest that his gun had been stolen but could be found if he "would go up to Benton Prairie."

This was indeed an odd comment, since Archie didn't own a gun. He had borrowed one from Fred True a few weeks before and fired one shot, supposedly at an alligator on the night Sam disappeared. It's also contradictory to the fact that Kate gave the gun back to True a week later, indicating that they had had it the entire time for protection.

We can understand what Archie was attempting with this comment about the gun when we consider the context. Benton's Prairie was, at this time, a largely black settlement about ten miles west of the Sanford area, near present-day Sorrento. It was the site of the first black public school in Orange County (1873).

Newspapers of the day often blamed robberies and various other unsolved crimes on blacks living in small communities on the fringes of towns and cities, so it's not entirely surprising that Archie tried to cast blame there by suggesting his own gun was involved but was stolen and in that community.

As if these comments weren't strange enough, Archie made one final, curious statement as they crested a hill overlooking McMillan's place: he told Saint that "McMillan's relations would get a good thing of it now since he was gone." Aside from being rather cold-hearted, it was conclusory, suggesting that Archie had personal knowledge of his fate and knew he would never come back.

OCTOBER 15

Two Old Watches

After Pichard, Saint and Tabor peered through the windows of Sam's house on Thursday morning, October 4, several other neighbors—whether serious about the whereabouts of Sam or simply curious about seeing the inside of the house of the reclusive miser—ventured onto the property and looked in the windows. They also poked around the barn and in the grove but found nothing. James Ingraham, who lent an air of authority to the searches, would later say in frustration that there had been so many people all over McMillan's property that they couldn't tell if any tracks or footprints were recent or what was what.

Despite his disappearance and the persistent rumors about foul play, a formal search of Sam's house was not conducted until October 15.

On that date, Edgar Harrison exercised his official capacity as constable and gathered Tabor, Dr. Moore, Zeri Adams and Charles Saint. This group had entered the house briefly on the morning of October 13 as the search party gathered outside and performed a cursory check to make sure Sam hadn't died from a fall or sickness.

On the fifteenth, they again entered the house with a key provided by Tabor (it wasn't made clear exactly how he came about this key) and carefully searched the entire house. But according to Harrison, the house appeared to be as Sam had last left it. Nothing was disturbed or out of place or missing. They searched two large storage trunks and an old leather satchel but did not find any money or anything of value; they only contained papers, books and two old watches.

They found no clues as to Sam's disappearance.

The next day, while sitting on the steps of Sawyer's Drug Store in town, Archie talked about Sam's disappearance with Constable Harrison. He asked if he (Harrison) thought they would find Sam's body. Harrison said that he initially thought they would find his body in the lake by now because "unless it was very heavily weighted, he would have raised up by this time." According to Harrison, Archie was curious about the science of that and prodded further: "He wanted to know of me what weight it would take to keep him under. I told him I was not prepared to answer his question fully, but I presumed it would require at least double his weight."

Newton then asked Harrison about the search of McMillan's house the day before and whether they found anything of value. Harrison said they had not. Archie specifically asked, "Did you happen to find two old watches?" Harrison was surprised and responded that they did in fact find two watches, "an old brass watch, and one silver watch."

Later that day, Archie also asked Dr. Moore about the search of McMillan's house and what they found and then commented to local merchant J.B. McGruder, "The neighbors said that McMillan had been murdered, and he didn't think so; he said he was a man who was just as likely to be gone three years to some foreign country and be back. He would turn up likely in three years."

There was, of course, no precedent for such a belief. None of Sam's friends ever knew him to disappear suddenly for even a few weeks without word, let alone years at a time, and there was no suggestion that he ever even traveled to a foreign country. He had been to the West once, but that was several years prior. He did go to his Deland property occasionally but usually told his neighbors and stayed only a few days. When he did make such a trip, he double locked his gate, secured his house and put all tools away under lock and key.

Archie's comment therefore stood in stark contrast to the facts and what everyone in the community knew about Sam and his habits. It also made Archie look more and more like the suspicious outsider, especially when Sam was found the next day.

OCTOBER 17

The Headless Miser

A second, larger search party commenced on Monday, October 17. The men again met at McMillan's and fanned out from there. This time, they were more desperate to find their friend and neighbor and moved with great deliberation through the orange trees, underbrush, lakeshore and footpaths.

Zeri Adams worked with the group who strung together fish lines with hooks attached to drag Lake Como. Two rowboats moved slowly together with the line between them to search the bottom. Archie participated in this part of the search but later disembarked and watched from shore.

The laborer Richard Cooper had mentioned a few days before that he had seen a large group of buzzards near some trees on the small island out in Crystal Lake, which adjoined Lake Como via two narrow channels.

Since Cooper lived at Mrs. Rawson's house on the west side of Crystal Lake, Edgar Harrison and Tony Fox walked there on October 17. Joined by two black men, they took a flat-bottomed boat and rowed out to the spot Cooper had identified.

Near some scrub growth, they saw an object that at first looked like a partially submerged tree stump. But as they got close, they saw it was a body "as if a person was standing up in the water."

Since the water was fairly shallow (three or four feet), Fox jumped out and waded toward the body. He immediately saw that it was headless and missing a leg. He also saw a rope tied around the waist, and when he pulled, a weighted burlap sack materialized from the murky bottom.

Harrison handed him a rope from the boat, and Fox tied it around the partially floating body. He climbed back into the boat, and they started to row, heading to Newton's landing on adjoining Lake Como. They towed the body and the weight behind.

At one point, passing though the shallow channel into Lake Como, they all had to get out of the boat and push it. Fox put the weighted burlap sack onto the boat's stern and actually held the mutilated decaying body in his arms while the others pushed. When they all had to carry the boat over a dry patch, he laid the body across the boat to help push and lift the boat.

After passing back into the lake, Fox put the body back into the water to be towed but kept the weight out for easier rowing. They continued this way all the way to the shore by Newton's house, the putrefying body lazily trailing along behind.

The body was in a deplorable state. The head was gone, as was most of the flesh of the neck. The top two vertebrae of the spine stuck out and hung loosely, barely attached to the column. The left side of the chest had a hole in it, and broken ribs and collarbone in that area were visible. The skin of the back was faded to a ghostly white with streaks of dye from the clothing.

There was a large opening in the abdomen just above the pelvis, and it turned out that all the organs of the body were missing except the lungs. One leg was hanging "simply by the ligamentous attachment"; the thigh of the other leg was denuded of flesh and had been severed from the knee down. Fox had found one of the shoes detached from the body—it contained the sole of the occupant's foot: the skin, muscle, tendons and bone were all completely gone.

Both hands were gone, the left forearm was missing and the right arm was badly mangled. All the witnesses said that what skin was left was hanging off the body in many places, and the decomposition was well along. It was

ADMINISTRATOR'S NOTICE,

All parties indebted to the late Samuel Mc-
Millan, will please come forward and settle said
indebtedness, and save litigation. All parties
having any claims against the late Samuel
McMillan, are hereby notified to present the
same within the time prescribed by law, or said
claims will be forever barred.

DAVID McMILLAN,
JOHN McMILLAN,
Administrators.

St. Clair-Abrams & Summerlin, Atl'ys said estate.
dec 28-8w,

Administrator's notice for the estate of Samuel McMillan. *Sanford Museum Collection.*

evident that while weighted down in the lake and then floating near the
surface, the body had been eaten by fish, turtles, birds and perhaps alligators.

As the men rowed toward shore with the mutilated body, they called out
and word spread. Several men searching the area around the lake gathered
on shore to watch the boat come in. Archie was in this group, and according
to Zeri Adams, he seemed very anxious about the prospect of seeing what
it towed. In fact, Adams would later testify that even before the boat landed
and the body removed to shore, Archie asked what it had been tied down
with and what was used as a weight.

7

ARRESTED

THE INQUEST

As the boat touched land, Edgar Harrison took charge of the official investigation of the body.

Originally from West Virginia, the forty-nine-year-old Harrison was one of the area's earliest and most respected settlers. He had moved his family to the Florida frontier from Paola, Kansas, in the early 1870s and settled in open country about ten miles from downtown Sanford, on its western edge. He called the area Paola after his time in Kansas, and the name stuck.

During his twenty-plus years in Paola, Florida, Harrison ran a successful general store, was named postmaster of Paola in July 1880 and served as the local justice of the peace and coroner. In these latter two capacities he is key to this part of our story.

In the 1880s, many cities and towns in America still used a loose system of sheriffs, constables, justices of the peace and local coroners to investigate and handle crime, especially in frontier and other developing areas. Most counties had an elected sheriff, but he was a one-man show, rarely had any formal staff and simply appointed local men as deputies or constables with minimum pay or bonuses that sometimes went unpaid. These men were the local authority, empowered to hear evidence, make arrests, levy fines for certain minor offenses, serve official papers and impose tax liens.

Sanford was in Orange County in 1882, and the county sheriff was T.W. Shine. But he was based in Orlando, about twenty-five miles and a long horseback ride to the south of Sanford. He had appointed Civil War veteran William Sirrine as constable for the city of Sanford, and Harrison had been appointed as a local justice of the peace and coroner for the outlying Paola/ Twin Lakes area.

So when the rotting headless body was dragged ashore on October 17, 1882, it was up to the local general store owner to determine who it was and what happened.

Harrison wasted no time. He began the formal coroner's inquest right there on the shore of Lake Como even before the canoe was tied up and the body dry. The search party and several others standing onshore—including Archie Newton—were officially called as witnesses and sworn in. Harrison would later testify that he was "pretty sure" he told the witnesses they had the right to refuse to answer any questions and didn't have to incriminate themselves as he examined the body and asked questions.

Tony Fox was ordered to cut the rope from the body and cut open the bag attached to it. He observed that the rope had several knots tied in it and was looped once around the body and twice around the heavy bag.

When he cut the bag open, the men could see a round container inside. Archie leaned forward with the others and said, "I think that looks like my pot." Fox reached in and removed a large iron pot; it was full of nails and quite heavy. As he set it on the ground for all to see, Archie said, "God! That's my pot." Everyone on the shore that day confirmed that Archie made this exclamation.

Archie probably regretted it as soon as the words left his mouth.

Constable Sirrine was present and removed the clothes from the body. He removed the coat (which he said was still buttoned fully) and shirt and cut off the undershirt. He removed the pants and noted that most of the pockets were turned inside out. He personally identified the coat (canvas with leather pockets) as one that was worn by McMillan "when he came to town" as a dress coat. He also recognized the shoes they found with the body: one shoe still had part of a foot in it, and the other was barely attached to the mutilated leg.

After removal of the clothes and inspection of the body on the muddy lakeshore in the shadow of the Newtons' house, Harrison adjourned his inquest until the next day, to be reconvened at his general store. The pot, bag, nails and rope were given to local lawyer Thomas Wilson by Harrison because he was present for the search and had a buggy to transport the items from the scene.

Zeri Adams went with Newton back to the house to inform Kate that the body had been found and it appeared to be Sam McMillan. Using language he characterized as "brutal or abrupt," Adams apparently did the talking and told Kate about finding the body and the terrible condition it was in. Archie interjected and referred to the body as "that damned thing." During the conversation, Archie looked at Kate in what Adams called "a fixed manner," which Adams undoubtedly took to be conspiratorial.

On October 18, Harrison again gathered the seven or eight men who were witnesses (including Archie) and empaneled a jury of peers to continue the inquest. Whether he was unsure of the official process or was just forgetful, Harrison would later testify that he *thought* he made a statement about their right to refuse to answer questions and not incriminate themselves. He was "satisfied" that Archie was present when he made these statements but couldn't be certain that he was in the room or heard him. Harrison stated that he had "bad eyesight" but didn't use glasses that day in his store so couldn't be sure he actually saw Archie in the room when this rather important announcement about constitutional rights was made.

Indeed, from all accounts about the inquest, it appears that Harrison failed to actually line up the witnesses, call their names for the record, affirmatively read their rights and get an acknowledgment.

This uncertainty about whether he notified the witnesses about what was by this time a basic American right is even more astounding given the fact that Thomas Wilson—a former prosecutor and prominent local lawyer—was present for the entire day and acted as clerk to record the testimony.

During the inquest, Harrison asked questions regarding McMillan's movements on Saturday, September 30, what the men had seen in the various searches and their own whereabouts during that time. He often referred to McMillan as "Sammy" and sometimes got confused about dates and times. Some of the jurors asked questions, but Wilson did not.

"THE MYSTERIOUS DISAPPEARANCE OF SAM'L MCMILLAN EXPLAINED"

The October 19, 1882 edition of the *South Florida Journal* reported the finding of the body with the headline "The Mysterious Disappearance of Sam'l McMillan Explained." It detailed the condition of the body and the probability that he had been murdered:

Mr. Harrison empanelled a jury and every endeavor is being made by the indignant citizens to ferret out the murderer, and we hope by next issue of the Journal *to have the satisfaction of chronicling the fact that the perpetrator of this heinous crime is in the hands of the law, and that conviction and punishment will quickly follow.*

After hearing all the witness statements, further examining the body and concluding that Sam was last seen alive at Archie and Kate's house, Harrison ultimately decided there was enough evidence to suspect and detain Mr. and Mrs. Newton until a formal preliminary hearing could be held. He ordered their detention and "turned the case over" to the constable on October 19. The Newtons were immediately taken into custody and held in Sanford to await the preliminary hearing, scheduled to start the next day.

The constable was Captain William Sirrine, a popular figure in Sanford. An ex-Confederate soldier, he was appointed justice of the peace and magistrate for this part of Orange County. He owned and operated the Sirrine House Hotel, a highly successful boardinghouse located on Palmetto Avenue right in downtown Sanford. A January 1883 article in *South Florida Journal* documented the popularity of the boardinghouse—two thousand visits from 1881 to 1882. In fact, Sirrine had to rent an additional building across the street to accommodate the volume of visitors to his popular establishment.

He also apparently took his role as local constable seriously; the *Sanford Journal* would later note in its Thursday, April 26, 1883 edition:

The judicial mill has been grinding quite actively for several days past, and Justice Sirrine, who so ably runs the machine, has been kept quite busy. The Justice presides with great dignity and ability, and his decisions are generally received with satisfaction. Sanford is peculiarly fortunate in having this important public service in the hands of one so competent and conscientious.

On October 19, 1882, Sirrine promptly issued a search warrant of the Newton house. A large group of men gathered at the property, with Edgar Harrison set to execute the warrant. He wasn't sure why so many people were there, however, and didn't really do anything to exclude or control the crowd. He also failed to list who went into the house and where they searched.

The Newtons were under detention in Sanford at the time, and their house was locked. Harrison had failed to get a key to conduct the search and didn't want to break in. Just as he was about to turn back, William Beardall stepped forward with a key to the house.

Recall that Beardall was the Englishman who two months earlier had accompanied Archie on a formal inspection of Sam's grove and whose presence changed Sam's mind about the seriousness of Archie as a buyer. Harrison would later say that he didn't even know why Beardall appeared at Newton's house that day and apparently didn't ask.

James Ingraham also was in attendance, as was R.L. Travis, who attended at the specific request of Archie Newton. Travis actually stayed with Harrison the entire time they searched, even though he had no official capacity and had not been deputized as a constable. Thomas Wilson also attended, ostensibly as an officer of the court.

This was actually the second search of the Newton house. Harrison had come the day before (he thought it was the day before) with a key from Captain Sirrine and did a cursory search with Dr. Moore, Emile Tissot, Tabor and Tony Fox in attendance. At least, that's who he could remember as attending. He wasn't really clear on why he did a first search and then a second and didn't seem to understand his official role in the handling of the criminal case.

It was during the second, more comprehensive search that they discovered some key evidence.

In the drawer of a bureau in the Newtons' bedroom, they found a gold ring in the right-hand pocket of a vest. The vest was Archie's. On the floor behind the leg of the bureau, several bankbooks were wedged against the wall. They also found some razors, assorted clothes and pants and several articles of "soiled" clothing in a trunk.

Most importantly, Harrison and his search party located a handkerchief with what looked like rust stains on its edges. Given the suspicion of murder now squarely laid on Kate and Archie, it wasn't difficult for the men to theorize that the stains were in fact human blood. They also found a skirt that was spattered with what Harrison characterized as "blood signs or rust."

Outside, they found a pile of nails under a corner of the house that some suspected matched the nails found in the pot that weighed down the body. Harrison said that there were finger marks in the sand around the nails, indicating that a man had reached down and scooped them up as if to put them into another container.

Suspicions were high, and these items were turned over to Captain Sirrine to be lined up as evidence for the criminal hearing. The *Florida Times Union* newspaper reported that "the people of Sanford were ablaze with excitement" about these developments and were most interested in seeing justice served.

But justice on the frontier also had a darker side, and newspaper accounts noted that "threats of lynching are numerous" but have "not been carried into effect." The men posted to detain Archie and Kate were armed and tasked not only to prevent their flight but also to protect them from a mob.

THE MISER'S HEAD

The proceeding that started on October 20 was essentially a preliminary criminal hearing, conducted to assess whether the evidence supported the findings of the inquest and the subsequent detention. If the constable decided it did, the defendants would be formally arrested and held in jail until the next court session convened; it would be then that a formal criminal trial would commence and their guilt or innocence determined. To bolster the case, Constable Sirrine and lawyer Thomas Wilson thought that finding McMillan's severed head was crucial, since it would provide dispositive proof that the mutilated body was indeed Sam McMillan. As the hearing started, they only had circumstantial evidence that this was in fact Sam McMillan, based mostly on the statements of friends and neighbors that the clothes looked like his. They also needed the head to confirm whether the victim had been shot in the head, whether the head had any evidence of being cut off with a razor (given Archie's request on October 1 to borrow a razor from Zeri Adams) and whether it too had been weighted down by the murderer.

Local residents J. Woodson and Andrew Middlemas were sent with some haste back out to Lake Como to search for the head. They started early the next day from McMillan's property and tried to find the "coon trap" that had been located during the first organized search on the thirteenth. They thought it was a shallow grave worthy of closer inspection for clues, but they could not locate it.

They continued to Newton's house and conducted a search "for a good while" of the grounds. They looked under the house, in the outside corners and around the barn. It does not appear that they entered the house (they had no permission to do so), but other visitors would later report that a back window had been broken and the house entered. This was never investigated or attributed to anyone.

Despite their effort, they found no head.

As the afternoon wore on, the intrepid searchers then took Archie's boat and rowed around Lake Como. They crossed into Crystal Lake, searched the shores and later rowed across to Mrs. Rawson's house. There, they located the laborer Richard Cooper and asked where exactly the body had been found. He pointed to the island of shrubs and partially submerged trees directly across and told them to look for the white cloth that Fox had tied to the closest tree.

They hurried to the spot in the boat and spent time carefully circling, scanning the water and the lake bottom for any clues.

They soon found Sam's head, submerged "in plain sight" according to the men, about twenty-five feet from where the body had been discovered weighted down a few days earlier.

Woodson swung out of the boat into the waist-deep water; he later estimated that it was three and a half feet deep at this point. He bent down and put his arms in the water, leaning forward to pick up the detached head. He says he was able to bend down and pick it up without getting his ears wet.

The head was resting crown up in the soft bottom of the lake. The lower jaw was detached and "lay a little ways off." The head was almost completely devoid of skin, showing the shiny white of the skull. When Woodson picked it up, he noticed that skin/flesh had pooled underneath on the lake floor, which made the water cloudy when he moved it. Not wanting to miss any potential evidence, he handed the dripping skull to Middlemas and bent back down to scoop up as much of the flesh as possible.

He also noticed small bits of what looked like paper scattered on the bottom of the lake and stooped again to scrape up a handful. Back on the boat, he noticed reddish hair in the material he had scooped, which he thought was from a beard or maybe the hair from a head.

Richard Cooper stood watching from shore, and since they were pressed for time, Middlemas explained how they asked for Cooper's help:

> *We hired him to row us to a grove on the east side* [of Crystal Lake] *near the railroad towards Sanford. We were in a hurry to get back to court and gave him $2.50 to take us across. We were afraid we would not get back in time.*

Clothing wet, their hands and faces streaked with dirt, a decaying head in a sack at their feet, they took the train back to Sanford to get to the hearing before it concluded. We can imagine the scene as they burst into the room where testimony was being heard and placed the sack with McMillan's severed head on the table for all to see.

CHARGED WITH MURDER

Unfortunately, we don't have any records from the proceedings, and no copies of any of the exhibits, letters, papers or evidence have survived. We do know that testimony was again presented about the pending sale of Sam's grove to Archie, Sam's last walk to the Newtons' place on the evening of September 30 and Archie's behavior thereafter, which included a large roll of cash and a lot of spending.

We also know from newspaper accounts that Sam McMillan's brothers David (from Salem) and John (from Webster City, Iowa) had arrived in Sanford. They both testified at the hearing about Sam's personal habits, what they knew about his orange grove (which wasn't much—the McMillan family wasn't especially close) and his personal effects. They were not able to identify the ring found in Archie's vest as one that belonged to their dead brother.

Archie's friend Fred True was a deputy constable and served as one of the guards. Perhaps trying to convince himself of his friend's innocence (or guilt), he talked privately to Archie throughout the proceedings. When he asked Archie why he said the pot of nails tied to McMillan's body was definitely his, Newton replied he thought it was "for the best." Kate, by this time extremely stressed about the whole affair, told Archie to "hush" and stop talking about it.

Despite his drinking problems, Zeri Adams was also enlisted as a deputy constable. In that role, he witnessed Kate have a panic attack in the middle of the night. She repeated "Oh my God. What shall I do?" over and over, so much so that Archie told Adams that she had gone crazy and "lost her mind."

It was so bad that Adams summoned a doctor, who examined her, prescribed medication and bed rest and diagnosed her with "neuralgia of the heart." This caused a several-day delay in the hearing so Kate could recover. It eventually went on without her.

On November 1, 1882, James Ingraham briefly updated Henry Sanford via letter about the hearing, noting that attorneys Abrams and Wilson, and Dr. L.M. Moore "and all of Sylvan Lake almost for the prosecution." Ingraham added, "We cannot believe he is guilty."

After what the newspapers called a "long and exhaustive examination before the justice of the peace," Archie Newton was charged with murdering Sam McMillan. He was formally arrested and sent to the Orange County jail on November 2, 1882. His request for bail was denied by Sirrine, and he would have to wait for the next term of the circuit court to determine his fate. Because court was not always in session at this time, Archie would have to wait until May 1883 for his trial.

But it seems the people of Twin Lakes and all of Sanford—from whom his jury pool would be drawn—already considered him guilty, according to the *South Florida Journal* on October 26, 1882:

> *It is believed that the fiend who committed the outrage chronicled in our last, has been captured and is now in jail. There may be some doubts as to his identity not yet removed, and this, likely, accounts for the quiet of the citizens of Orlando. As we have heard the reasons for believing the captured party the guilty one, there is but little doubt, if any, that he is. We have no suggestions to make, but await the results.*

Archie's benefactor Sir William MacKinnon was informed of Archie's arrest and, in February 1883, wrote about it to Henry Sanford:

> *As you can imagine I am much grieved by the position of the poor youth Newton. He is not yet 22 I believe, and it is difficult to believe he can have jumped into such crime so suddenly.*

But there are no records showing that MacKinnon or Sanford did anything specific to help Archie.

8

TRIAL BY JURY

THE JAIL

By the time the murder trial started at the end of May 1883, Archie had been sitting in jail for almost six months. As you may have guessed, prisons in frontier towns in the 1880s were not pleasant. Hot and crowded, they had little ventilation or comforts. Neither air conditioning nor running water was available, of course, so we can imagine how horrible conditions were in a squat brick or heavy wood structure with few windows.

The Orange County jail was no different. It was made of hewn logs, had a stout wall enclosing the yard and boasted a fine lock on the door. Considered very secure, the inside was covered in rough-hewn wood planks, and a small living quarters for the jailor sat outside. It seemed to have constantly needed repair, and there were frequent makeshift additions of cells and rooms and many complaints about its sanitary condition.

There are no records showing exactly where the jail was located. Many historians think it was situated either on the southwest corner of Court and Wall Streets or on the west side of Orange Avenue, across from the end of Wall Street.

But late nineteenth-century convicts often didn't sit in a prison cell. Orange County commissioners had ordered in 1876 that the sheriff was permitted to use county convicts for county work. He was authorized to "hire out said Convicts at 25 cts. per day and their Board, first taking good and sufficient

Downtown Orlando, Florida, circa 1880, site of Archie Newton's murder trial. *State Archives of Florida.*

security for their Safe Keeping." Such "safekeeping" often entailed use of a caged wagon that served as transport and sometimes overnight quarters for the prisoners. The use of convicts as hired labor was a common practice in Florida and other parts of the South, not only to save taxpayer money but also generate revenue. Given conditions at the time, the sheriff wasn't concerned about the prisoners' morale or allegations of mistreatment.

There are no records as to whether Archie was used in this way as forced labor. It's possible, given his notoriety and family background, that he was spared this aspect of frontier justice and left to a cell. Or it's possible this made him more of a target.

We also don't know if he was given a private jail cell or any amenities, again given his station. We don't know whether Kate was allowed to visit and if so, how often, where they were allowed to meet, if she could bring food or if she could handle correspondence for him. It's not clear if Kate stayed in Orlando during the timeframe from November 1882 to May 1883 or continued to live in their Twin Lakes home. The trip back and forth to Sanford would have been several hours by horseback in the harsh Florida heat and a little under an hour on the South Florida Railroad line, which by now connected the two towns.

There also was the specter of public hanging, which was used to punish capital crimes such as murder and rape. Archie would have known that just two years earlier, in 1880, Henry Stokes had become the first legally convicted criminal hanged at a public execution in Orange County. The prosecutor had been none other than Alexander St. Clair Abrams, who would rack up seventy criminal trials in his six-year stint as prosecutor, with fifty-three guilty verdicts. He was already pushing for execution in Archie's case.

By law, execution was one of the duties of the sheriff in that time period, and Captain Shine likely had already sized Archie up for the noose.

COURTHOUSE

The Orange County Courthouse loomed a few dusty streets over from the jail. Built in 1875, it was situated on Central Avenue at the exact center of Orlando.

It was a wood frame structure, with two main floors and a third affectionately called the attic (where the petit jury was forced to meet). The large main courtroom (reportedly seating five hundred spectators) was on the second floor; the clerk and other administrative offices were on the first floor, along with the records storage and a brick vault enclosing the most secure of safes for the storage of the county's valuables.

The courthouse was the center of community life for the Orlando town and the county. In addition to the administration of justice and county business, it was used for church services, lodge meetings, political gatherings, brass band practice and even as a skating rink. The Benevolent Dramatic Association of Orange County was allowed to build a stage in the courtroom for performances.

At this time, both Orlando and Sanford sat in Orange County, which encompassed a large swath of Central Florida. From 1870 to 1875, most legal and county business was conducted in Sanford itself, as it was the larger of the two and sat on the key transportation hub.

But in 1875, the much smaller crossroad cattle town of Orlando was selected as the county seat, over the strident objections of Henry Sanford. Despite his connections and influence, and despite the fact that his town as

NO. 125 PANORAMIC VIEW, ORLANDO FLA. LOOKING E.
125

Orange County Courthouse at the time of Archie's trial. *State Archives of Florida.*

a prime transportation and traffic hub was better suited for the center of government, Sanford miscalculated the will of the locals.

When the issue of where to build the county's courthouse came up in 1875 (which would centralize the county's operations), local leaders cast about for money to build it. A rich cattle baron named Jacob Summerlin lived in Orlando and purportedly offered a $10,000 "loan" to the county if the courthouse was built near his estate. He was tired of making the arduous two- to three-hour trip by horseback up to Sanford on a regular, sometimes daily basis to conduct his business. Summerlin's loan had generous repayment terms as well as language that said it really didn't have to be paid back at all.

Henry Sanford's offer had been much smaller. His city had significantly more registered voters than Orlando, and he thought his electorate would easily select his town as the county seat. Characteristically, he was imperious and refused to negotiate further.

He was wrong.

With what has been described as a clever combination of well-placed money and free alcohol, Summerlin engineered a large "get out the vote" campaign and won the selection of Orlando as the county seat. Plans for the

Orange County Courthouse. *State Archives of Florida.*

courthouse were selected, money changed hands and the courthouse rose from the dusty streets of downtown Orlando, never to leave.

In a way, the courthouse built in 1875 was the symbol of Sanford's defeat and would mark the ascendency of Orlando. This fact would not have been lost on all of the witnesses and participants from Sanford, Twin Lakes and Paola who were forced to trudge to Orlando in June 1883 for Archie's trial.

THE LAWYERS

Archie survived his time in the Orlando jail. When he finally sat at the defense table at the start of his trial in May 1883, he was flanked by one of the best-known lawyers in Florida, Eleazar K. Foster Jr.

Foster was the son of an esteemed Connecticut lawyer and state legislator. He went to Yale, receiving his undergraduate degree at the height of the Civil War in 1863. He took a year off for an illness (rather than enlisting in the army), then went to Yale Law School and was admitted to the bar in spring 1865, just as General Grant accepted Lee's surrender at Appomattox.

In poor health much of his life, Foster moved to St. Augustine, Florida, in 1866 for the warm weather. Through family connections, he was appointed port tax collector and then made U.S. attorney for the Fourth Judicial District

Eleazar K. Foster, Archie Newton's lead defense attorney. *Manuscripts and Archives. Yale University Library.*

of Florida in 1868. But he resigned two years later because of ill health and moved to Sanford just as Henry Sanford starting laying out the town boundaries and building roads. A letter from Foster Sr. to Sanford recommended the junior Foster for legal advice and counsel in the establishment of the town.

He settled in as a local lawyer, grew his political connections and proved himself smart and capable. In 1895, the *Ocala Evening Star* referred to Foster as "one of the brainiest lawyers in Florida or anywhere else."

In 1881, he was appointed state superintendent of public instruction (the modern-day equivalent to secretary of education) and seems to have split much of his time between the state capital in Tallahassee and Sanford. In taking the job, Foster was described as "a lawyer by profession, in habits of mind and inclination, and doubtless occupied the office at great financial loss to himself and at a sacrifice of his personal preferences."

He seems to have been rather successful in this role, instituting sweeping change to public education in Florida: he made it a misdemeanor for school officers and teachers to deal in textbooks or to be agents of publishers, he changed the system of appointing school boards and gave county superintendents power to revoke teachers' certificates (for "intemperance" or "immorality"). Foster also established an institute for the deaf and mute.

But he resigned his position before the end of its term because of (you guessed it) ill health.

In January and February 1883, as Archie sat in jail in Orlando, it appears Foster was in Tallahassee nearly full time while the legislature met. It's not clear how much time he took during this busy two-month period to prepare the defense of Archie Newton or how much correspondence he had with his client. But the trial date was fast approaching.

Foster and Archie faced a formidable prosecutor across the aisle in Alexander St. Clair Abrams. Known as the "Volcanic Creole," Abrams was

Alexander St. Clair Abrams, the prosecutor. *Lake & Sumter Style.*

from New Orleans and had served as a private in the Confederate army. He was at the Siege of Vicksburg but was discharged in September 1862 because of illness. Trapped in the city, he wrote detailed reports of daily life and the military goings-on and published them as a novel in 1864 (*The Trials of the Soldier's Wife*).

Later paroled, Abrams moved to Atlanta, where he became a newspaper reporter. When Atlanta was besieged by Sherman in 1864, he took up arms in its defense, was wounded and discharged. After the war, Abrams moved to New York and inexplicably became foreign editor for the *New York Herald*. By 1870, he kept rooms at the Astor House in downtown New York and held the key to encrypted cables from around the world.

But his health later failed, and he moved back to Atlanta to start his own newspaper (the *Daily Herald*). Not surprisingly, his sensationalistic New York journalism style didn't work in the Deep South. When it folded, he moved to Florida to practice law.

Sometimes referred to as "major," it doesn't appear that he was ever anything more than a private in the Confederate army—and only briefly at that. He has been described as "an egotist of the first order" and as an "ambitious, irascible, and unscrupulous man who had married wealth" and was determined to show it to everyone.

And he was determined to convict Archie Newton.

PRELIMINARY MANEUVERS

The presiding judge was W. Archer Cocke. He was a no-nonsense, "get to justice" kind of judge, and he wanted this trial to start.

He ordered Archie to appear on May 22, 1883, to be formally arraigned.

The indictment was read to a crowded courtroom, no doubt excited to get a look at the young Englishman and his wife and get on with what most assumed would be an easy guilty verdict. The charges detailed the multiple violent methods that Archie allegedly used to kill his neighbor Sam McMillan.

Trial was ordered to begin on May 28.

However, there was a problem. In a pretrial hearing on May 25, the court found that "a sufficient number of jurors cannot be obtained to serve as jurors" from the regular panel of names already drawn. Judge Cocke ordered Sheriff Shine's brother, who was clerk of courts, to "draw the names of one hundred persons to serve as jurors in said cause from the list of 300 selected by the county Commissioners" for 1883.

But Shine couldn't find enough people from the list. That's because Archie's murder trial wasn't the only game in town. There were *two* other capital cases going on at the exact same time, in the same courthouse, before the same

Judge Cocke. In addition to Archie
Newton, Silas Carter was charged with
a murder that occurred a few months
earlier, and a young black man, Arthur
Williams, was charged with rape.

Most of the daily administrative and
scheduling aspects of court proceedings
from this time were recorded in the
Orange County Court Minute Book.
Fortunately, the original book survived
on a dusty shelf until the 1960s, when
some enterprising soul had the foresight
to transfer it to microfilm. The film
then sat in a storage room for three
more decades before it was discovered
by an attorney who came across it as
he researched the early legal history of
Orange County. Since then, he stored
the film in the stuffy attic of his cabin

Judge Archer Cocke, who presided
over Archie Newton's trial. *State
Archives of Florida.*

in North Carolina and was kind enough to share it.

These records help us track the proceedings in which the lives of these
three men were at stake. They show that the murder trial of Silas Carter
lasted only a few days, and Arthur Williams's trial for rape commenced on
May 29 and lasted only one day.

In fact, when the jury was sent out to deliberate Arthur's fate, Archie
Newton was ordered in to the courtroom to enter his formal plea.

But through his lawyer, E.K. Foster, Archie instead entered a plea in
"abatement." This was a procedural maneuver used to delay the proceedings
and preserve other arguments about the case. Court was adjourned until 3:00
p.m. At that time, just as the hottest part of the Florida summer descended
upon the courtroom, the Arthur Williams jury came back and announced a
guilty verdict; he was sentenced to hang and taken out.

Judge Cocke then immediately brought Archie back in and heard the
following motion by Foster:

> *The said Archibald W. Newton in his own proper person cometh into and
> having heard the indictment read to him, saith that said indictment should
> abate and the State of Florida ought not further to prosecute said indictment
> because it was found by an illegally constituted Grand Jury. In this, that*

*the Grand Jury who found said indictment and brought the said indictment
into court, had never been legally drawn and summoned.*

This motion was based on a recent change of the court's term and Sheriff
Shine's failure to complete the proper paperwork about serving the grand
jurors he did call. But Judge Cocke wasn't in the mood and summarily
denied the motion to dismiss the case.

Archie stood and formally entered a plea of not guilty.

Foster then immediately asked Judge Cocke to postpone the trial so he
could interview three additional witnesses, whose testimony was "material
and necessary to his defense." These witnesses were Thomas Bennett of
New Haven, Connecticut, who worked for the Winchester Repeating
Arms and Cartridge Company; Horace Lord of Hartford, Connecticut,
a representative of Colt Arms Manufacturing Company; and Thomas
Bowron, who resided in Hull, England, and was Kate Newton's brother.

To support his request, he provided a summary of what he thought each
witness would attest to but told the judge that they needed to be interviewed
in person, especially Bowron (who, Foster said, would provide crucial
testimony about holding a large amount of money for Kate Newton that
could have been used to buy McMillan's grove). Because of the distance and
travel expense for each, he needed more time.

No doubt frustrated by these delay tactics and because it was now late in
the day and hot in the courtroom, Judge Cocke adjourned until the next day.

On June 1, court was called to order, and the judge told the crowd that
he was granting Foster's motion and would postpone the trial. They were
stunned and probably a bit let down that the drama of the trial would not
be starting. This was the third or fourth time in the past two weeks that the
crowd had packed into the gallery only to be sent home.

But prosecutor Abrams was prepared for this possibility. He stood and
told Judge Cocke that he would admit that the three witnesses would say
what Foster thought they would say. As such, Abrams concluded—perhaps
with a sly smile—there was now no reason to postpone the trial and the state
was ready to begin.

Judge Cocke was conflicted. He had ruled to postpone the trial, and judges
don't like to change their minds. So he did the only prudent thing possible:
he banged his gavel and adjourned until later in the day.

We can imagine the buzz in the courtroom as everyone filed out and
picture the dozens of small groups talking in the hallway and stairwell and
front lawn about what had just happened.

At 2:30 p.m., court reopened, and Judge Cocke reversed himself. He agreed with Abrams that since the state admitted to the facts of the three witnesses, their actual testimony was no longer necessary. He denied Foster's motion to postpone the trial with finality.

But he had thought further about the juror problem and also decided to quash the jury pool that had been assembled. He instead issued a new order to Sheriff Shine to go out and summon fifty *more* people from the "body of the county at large" to serve as potential jurors in the Newton case.

Given the multiple delays in the case and perhaps because of his earlier failure to find enough people, Sheriff Shine wasted no time. He paraded fifty souls into the courtroom later that day and presented them to the judge. Because of challenges and disqualifications, however, only four of the fifty were ultimately empanelled. Judge Cocke ordered Sheriff Shine to go out and get another one hundred men and told everyone to come back on Monday morning June 4.

On June 4, the spectators again filled the courtroom, hoping for the show to finally start. But Sheriff Shine reported that he was not able to find one hundred people as ordered. Moreover, one of the four jurors who already had been selected reported that his child died the night before. Frustrated but probably sympathetic, Judge Cocke postponed the trial to Thursday, June 7.

Archie was sent out, and the court addressed other pending criminal cases. Judge Cocke then moved on to the civil cases pending in his court. Curiously, two of those civil cases involved Alexander St. Clair Abrams: both appear to be breach-of-contract cases in which Abrams sought damages of $10,000 in one and $20,000 in the other.

The defendant in both? Henry Sanford.

This reinforces the audacity of Abrams and his potential conflict of interest regarding Archie, especially when we see that the lawsuits stemmed from attempts by Abrams to get hired by Sanford as his lawyer for what looked to be a lucrative land deal in the Everglades. Most people believed that both coasts of Florida would soon be developed, tamed with railroads and settled. Land speculation hopes were running high, and Abrams no doubt wanted a piece.

But a professional relationship with Sanford and the Florida Land and Colonization Company never materialized, and Sanford looked elsewhere. Abrams, not one to let a good argument fall away, sued for the fees and profits he *would* have made had Sanford hired him. Indeed, Sanford's papers contain several letters about the "Abrams suit" for the next two years as it wound its way through the court.

These allegations show the acrimony and ongoing feuds that then existed between Abrams and Sanford. It also perhaps suggests an undertone of hostility toward Archie Newton, who would have been painted with the same Henry Sanford brush by Abrams.

THE CASE AGAINST ARCHIE NEWTON

Abrams's civil lawsuits were continued, and the court further addressed the lack of juror problem when it reconvened on June 7 at 11:00 a.m. It was ninety-eight degrees outside and even hotter inside the courtroom; one attendee wrote in his diary that "it is the warmest I ever saw here."

Much to the relief of everyone in attendance fanning themselves and hoping for some breeze, Sheriff Shine came in and announced that he had finally rounded up one hundred men as ordered. They were called in and sworn, and the lawyers spent the rest of the day questioning them, disqualifying some, excusing others and finally empanelling a complete jury of twelve men.

The trial of Archie Newton got underway at 9:00 a.m. on Friday, June 8, 1883. One witness (Harry True) remarked that by the time the trial started, he hadn't heard talk of anything but the McMillan case for the last four or five months. This was indeed a big event.

In American jurisprudence, the prosecution has the burden to prove that the defendant is guilty beyond any reasonable doubt. Any question about what happened, about the evidence or any element of the crime must be resolved in favor of the defendant. A guilty verdict cannot be rendered if there are doubts about what happened or about the defendant's involvement.

To overcome reasonable doubt, prosecutors—both now and in the 1880s—work to establish three main things: motive, means and opportunity.

In this case, Archie had a motive: he wanted to buy Sam's orange grove and may or may not have had the money to do it. He also had the means to commit the crime: he admitted to borrowing a gun from Fred True, he had the gun at the time of Sam's disappearance, and the chamber of the gun showed that a shot had been fired when returned to True.

And perhaps most damaging, Archie had the opportunity: Sam was last seen walking to Archie's house (with Archie at his side no less), and both Newtons admitted to having Sam over for tea on the night he disappeared.

Front page ads in the *Sanford Journal* newspaper, showing some of the major players in the McMillan murder. *Sanford Museum Collection.*

Although Abrams could show these three things, he lacked the one crucial thread to tie them together and remove all reasonable doubt: direct evidence.

There was no eyewitness to the crime and no direct evidence that Archie had done it. The use of fingerprints as a method of identification was still a decade or so away, and the body had been submerged in water so long that any evidence was long gone, either washed away, dissolved or eaten by lake creatures. Neither Archie nor Kate confessed to the crime, and none of the money they spent in the weeks following Sam's disappearance was examined for comparison to bills possessed by Sam.

So Abrams did what any skilled lawyer would do—he relied almost entirely on circumstantial evidence. In fact, this was the only evidence he had. And he made effective use of it.

He first took the unusual approach of presenting the state's case in a chronological fashion. That is, witnesses were called in accordance with the timeline of actual events and only gave testimony for that part of the story. Witnesses are usually called to the stand once and asked about all they know, whether they were involved in the first part of the story, the end, the middle, different parts and so on. This makes it easier on the witnesses and allows the jury to assess each witness's version of events and credibility in its totality.

In Newton's trial, however, individual witnesses were called to the stand numerous times, some as many as six different times depending where in the story and timeline of events Abrams was and what part the witness played in it.

Sam's neighbor J.O. Tabor was the first witness called. Abrams started with Tabor to lay out the background: Sam's peculiarities, the fact that he carried large sums of money on his person, his desire to sell the orange grove and his interaction with Archie Newton. This was the first mark on the timeline that would lead to his disappearance, the desperate searches, Archie's behavior and his ultimate arrest.

To this point, I've told you most of this story from the pages of the trial transcript itself, which tracked Abrams's approach and contained much detail. This information came out through the testimony of the witnesses, and where possible, I've given you several direct quotes and Q/A exchanges so you can read the actual voices of the people and hear things directly from them, in their own words.

You've heard most of the story already, and you know the players, the issues, the background. Now I want to put you in the jury box in that hot, stuffy courtroom. Discern whether some of the witnesses have their own motives and biases. Consider whether Archie and Kate's actions in the weeks following McMillan's disappearance, especially with money, were unusual.

Listen to prosecutor Abrams present his case, and consider the eight items he introduced as key pieces of evidence.

Above all, ladies and gentlemen, decide whether Archie Newton killed Sam McMillan on September 30, 1882.

ITEM NO. 1

The Skull

McMillan's head was discovered on October 21, 1882, in about three and a half feet of water in Crystal Lake. You'll recall that this was during the preliminary criminal hearing against Archie, and much urgency was placed on finding the head.

J.H. Woodson and Andrew Middlemas pulled the head from the water, scooped up a few handfuls of flesh from the lake bottom and rushed the head to the authorities in Sanford. They burst into the hearing and handed the sack with Sam's head to Captain Sirrine.

Sirrine testified that he opened the sack and removed the head, which was in a "very filthy condition," the inside "filled with rottenness, putrid." The hearing room had a "crowd" of people who pressed in to see the head, and they all must have recoiled at the smell.

Local physician Dr. F.A. Caldwell was called in to examine the skull and render his opinion as to the cause of death. To aid in his examination, Sirrine got two barrels, laid several boards across them and covered it with a sheet or cloth to form a makeshift morgue table.

Dr. Caldwell said that the skull was completely bare and had a ragged, oblong hole near the large foramen at the base of the skull. The hole was not natural and had been caused by being struck with a "pronged instrument" or "the entry of a bullet."

When he turned the skull over, Dr. Caldwell found the brain matter to be in a "softened condition" and "very decomposed" after sitting in the lake for several weeks. He punctured the lining so that he could examine the brain itself, and then shook the skull to get some of the material to come out onto the cloth. He then took a wire and "got it all out"; while doing so, he discovered a leaden bullet:

Q: Did you see the bullet?
A: Of course, I took it out.

[Mr. Abrams stated that he would be compelled to have Mr. Sirrine, the custodian of the bullet, present while it was being examined, as Mr. Sirrine would not identify it if it went out of his possession.]

By the Court: Let him come in, but as it is the practice to separate witnesses, I don't like to do it.
Mr. Sirrine here came into court and handed the witness the bullet.

Q: Do you recognize that bullet?
A: Yes.

Q: Where did that bullet come from?
A: From this skull.

Q: State to the jury how it came out.
A: I had removed the brain, had not removed it entirely, but I shook the skull and could hear something rattling in there and I shook it out and it dropped on the barrel or floor.

Sirrine added later that he had encouraged Dr. Caldwell to "shake it hard" so that whatever was rattling inside would come out: "He turned it around so and the bullet dropped." Sirrine demonstrated how he had put the boards across the barrels and laid a cloth over them. He then mimicked the motions he and the doctor had employed in turning the skull and shaking the bullet out.

Throughout this testimony, Abrams held the skull up dramatically for the jury. He handed it to Dr. Caldwell and asked several questions about the proximity of the gun to make such a hole, each time having the doctor physically point to the hole and hold up the skull.

Dr. Caldwell concluded that the gun had either been at close or "medium" range but couldn't be sure. He later said "no more than a foot away," but neither lawyer pressed him on the actual distance and he wasn't a forensic specialist. Neither he nor any other expert had examined the inside of the skull for evidence, and no other experts were used for examining the angle of the bullet's entry.

Abrams did ask Dr. Caldwell about the position of the head when the bullet was fired. He asked whether "the wound could be inflicted by a shot at a head laying that way" and theatrically laid his head on his hands, resting on a table. He also stooped in at least two different positions and held himself like a "stoop shouldered man" while he asked the doctor questions.

It turns out that the good doctor did not examine the inside of the skull itself and didn't check to see where the bullet had been lodged or what path it took across the brain from the entry point in the rear. He didn't take any notes or make any diagrams and was unsure of the date of his exam or who was present, despite the fact that he had conducted his examination as part of a formal criminal proceeding. He simply showed up when summoned, looked at the skull, scraped out the brain matter, shook the skull, shook it again harder and that was that.

The skull was an important piece of evidence, and things got testy at several points regarding the skull. When Charles Saint was on the stand to help identify the skull as Sam's by its lack of upper teeth, the following exchange occurred:

> Q: I want you to state if you can whether or not he was a man with the usual number of teeth allotted to us?
>
> By Mr. Foster: He testified to that before.
> By Mr. Abrams: I want him to testify to it again. Before he merely referred to it incidentally.
> By the Court: You can simply ask him to explain his testimony and you can offer in evidence the skull.
> By Mr. Foster: There should be an end to this recalling.
> By Mr. Abrams: That end will be when the State says "We close."
>
> * * *
>
> The skull and lower jaw were here placed in evidence.
> As also the pieces of paper with the fragments of hair.

By these rather simple references, the court reporter notes for us that after the testimony and heated exchanges about Sam's skull, the jury was able to view and hold the skull and closely examine the fragments of hair and small bits of paper scooped by hand from the lakebed.

ITEM NO. 2

The Six-Shooter

Next to the skull, the gun that may have been the murder weapon was the most important piece of evidence. Its handling and testing before trial, however, is shocking even by late nineteenth-century legal standards.

Archie's friend Fred True said he loaned his Colt double-action .38 revolver to Archie sometime between September 10 and 15, 1882. He said that Newton had requested it "to protect himself or some such reason." He didn't see the gun again until the night Archie was arrested, when Kate gave it back to him and indicated that it had been kept under their pillow the entire time.

On the witness stand, True testified that the gun was a six-shooter, but there were only four cartridges in the chamber when he loaned it to Archie:

> *Q: Did you or* [did you] *not say anything to him about firing it off?*
> *A: I gave it to him and showed him how to use it, and asked him not to fire it off unless he was obliged to.*

> *Q: Why?*
> *A: I never had but 4 cartridges and there was some difficulty in getting more.*

Prosecutor Abrams then asked about the conversation True had with Archie on October 1, the day after Sam's disappearance:

> *Q: Did he say anything about the pistol you had loaned him?*
> *A: He said that he had shot off the evening before or that day.*

> *Objection, leading questions.*

> *By the Court: Ask him what he said about the pistol.*

> *Q: Go on?*
> *A: He said he shot it off the evening before or that morning at an alligator. I am not certain which.*

> *Q: Did he state how many shots were fired?*
> *A: He did not.*

Q: When you received the pistol from the hands of Mrs. Newton, you say there were but 3 full cartridges in it?
A: Yes.

Q: What did you do with that pistol?
A: I gave it to C.A. Fox.

Q: Known as "Toney"?
A: Yes.

(Justice Sirrine here walked into court and handed Mr. Abrams a pistol.)

Q: Look at that pistol (handing to witness).
A: Where is the sight?

Q: I haven't the least idea.
A: There was a little piece cut out of the underside of the left hand side of the sight, and that is the way I would recognize it again. The sight is broke off, but then inside there is a piece broke off. It looks like my pistol.

(Witness here took the pistol to pieces and put it back again.)

It works better than it did when I had it. If the sight was on it, I could tell in a minute. There was a little piece cut out under it. The sight was on it when I loaned it to him.

By Mr. Sirrine, speaking up: I have the sight in my pocket and can explain how it came out.

Mr. Foster: We object. Mr. Sirrine is not on the stand.

By the witness: Yes that's my pistol.

Q: How do you know it?
A: There are two pieces at the end of the dog that are broke off. Then there is a small piece of wire that comes down to meet these 2—that's broke off too.

Q: You swear that is your pistol?
A: Yes.

Q: You swear that is the pistol you loaned to Newton?
A: Yes.

This chaotic scene undoubtedly rattled the lawyers and the courtroom audience. It certainly cast doubt on the reliability of the state's evidence (regarding the gun and all the other evidence it had stored) and whether it even had produced the correct gun.

Sirrine would later be called to the stand and asked about the broken piece. He said that the sight came off while he was "crowding it into a cigar box in which I carried it." He simply broke the sight off while pushing the gun into a box. But he added helpfully, "I have it in my pocket," and produced it for Abrams and the jury while on the witness stand.

Unfortunately, the tortuous journey of the broken sight wasn't done, as the court reporter then noted: "In passing sight to the jury, it fell in the sawdust but was subsequently uncovered."

But Sirrine wasn't done with surprising everyone with his handling of the evidence. On cross-examination by Foster, he said:

Q: Is that pistol, with the exception of the missing sight in the same condition it was when you received it?
A: With the exception of the ball taken out, and the ball fired out, and except I found it rusty and had it cleaned.

Rather than simply keep the gun secure for later examination—which was his role—he *cleaned* it. Forensic science admittedly wasn't that advanced in 1883, but this act certainly removed any evidence that might have existed on or in the gun and rendered useless any future testing. In fact, cleaning the gun arguably changes the nature of the entire piece, from the inside of the barrel, the action of the chamber, the function of the hammer and the way the projectiles move through it.

It also calls into question the methods of the law enforcement and court officers in this case and gives rise to questions about the motives of those charged with investigating and prosecuting crime. There is no outward evidence of bias in the record, but the way several key players so blithely handled and regarded the evidence is striking.

And yes, there is more. Sirrine also revealed this gem for the jury:

Q: At the time it was handed to you, how many cartridges did it contain?
A: 3 loaded cartridges and 1 empty cartridge shell.

Q: (opening the chamber of pistol) I notice in this 4 shells and only 1 loaded cartridge. You say there were 3 loaded cartridges when you took it. What became of the other 2?
A: One of them in examining the pistol the day after it was handed to me accidentally discharged and the bullet went into my window sill.

Q: Have you got the piece of window sill it went into?
A: Yes. (Handing piece of wood)

Q: Where is the bullet?
A: In here I suppose.

Q: Take it out?
(Witness cut bullet out of the wood)

A: Here is the bullet.

Q: Account for the other bullet?
A: The other one, I ordered the pistol opened for Mr. Grohman to have it forced through the barrel to see if it made the same kind of a twist that appeared to be on the ball that was found in the skull.

Q: Where is that bullet?
A: It is in my pocket (showing it).

Q: Were you present at that experiment?
A: I was.

Q: Will you swear that was the bullet?
A: That is the bullet, that is the other.

It's comical to picture the state's key law enforcement officer—who investigated the crime and initially charged Archie Newton with murder—explain that he accidentally shot off the murder weapon into his own windowsill. It's more comical still that he had the piece of sill with him, produced it out of thin air and was asked to dig the bullet out on the witness stand while everyone watched.

After this debacle of evidence handling, Sirrine went on to describe the ballistics test he performed with a local gunsmith named John Grohman, who had moved to Sanford just before Sam's disappearance and ostensibly wouldn't have had any bias one way or the other.

Grohman and Sirrine inspected the barrel of the gun and opened the chamber. They intended to test to see if another bullet made the same markings as the one shaken loose from the skull. This at least was a good forensic method based on solid scientific reasoning.

But not to be outflanked by sound reasoning, the men decided to clean the barrel first because it was dirty and "rusty." Then, they decided not to fire the gun (which would be the best way to compare the effects of the rifling on the bullet); instead, they slowly forced it down the barrel with a long pin or rod. (Sirrine wasn't sure which it was.)

This obviously didn't generate the same velocity as firing the bullet would have. It certainly wouldn't have produced the same spin, at the same speed, as if fired, and likely would not produce the same markings. Its reliability as a forensic test was almost nil and should have rendered the entire process inadmissible.

Judge Cocke even got in on the fun here and asked his own question from the bench: "Will a ball forced through a pistol lose more of its original weight than a ball shot through?" The expert really wasn't sure.

Undoubtedly trying to recover from Sirrine's bumbling, Abrams went dramatic again and opened a brand new box of bullets, explaining the contents with fanfare as he did so, "38 calibre long center fire metallic cartridges, manufactured by the Winchester Repeating Arms Company of New Haven, Connecticut USA." He pulled out several cartridges as he questioned the gunsmith Grohman about bullet weights, powder measurements and bullet types.

Abrams asked the gunsmith to weigh the bullet from True's gun and then weigh two cartridges taken from the box of Winchester cartridges he had opened for the jury. This comparison, he apparently hoped, would connect the bullet from True's .38 caliber six-shooter to the standard bullet types for that weapon, and thus connect the gun to the murder.

Grohman weighed the bullet from True's gun, wiped off lubricant from the two new cartridges and got different weights for all three. He was cross-examined extensively about the accuracy of his scale and his ability to calculate weights and convert them between English and American weight scales but wasn't all that convincing.

Grohman then revealed that he actually had never tested his scales for accuracy or had them calibrated with the current standards. Ever.

Immediately after Grohman stepped down, Abrams called T.E. Price, a druggist from Orlando who purportedly was an expert at weighing things. He was asked to test the various bullets with his own scale, ostensibly to reinforce Grohman's findings.

This strategy failed miserably.

Price got a variety of results, many of which differed from what Grohman had just found on his set of scales.

It was then revealed that Price used a few small slivers of paper in one of the scale pans of his own scale, to balance them. But he had no idea what the paper itself weighed and had not factored that into any of his answers.

The judge ordered the courtroom windows closed because the gentle breeze may have impacted operation of the scales, affecting accuracy. It also prevented the druggist from testing the weight of the paper he was using as ballast.

Things came to a dramatic and hectic conclusion when the bullet that was removed from the remaining cartridge in True's gun was weighed again by both experts. Grohman announced the weight as 146 grams. Looking over his shoulder, Abrams blurted, "He makes a mistake—it is 145 grams." Foster rebuked him by saying, "Don't tell him." Abrams then pulled cartridge after cartridge out of the box of new ones and had the men weigh bullet after bullet. All had slightly different weights no matter who weighed them, and Abrams's strategy crumbled.

When the battle of the dueling weights was done, Abrams had failed badly. No one could say for sure what a bullet taken from True's gun weighed, and no one could really match the gun to the spent bullet taken from McMillan's skull.

It's unfathomable that a key piece of evidence such as the murder weapon itself would be so mishandled—a piece broken, the barrel cleaned, a shot accidentally fired, weights and measures so confused and haphazard—but still introduced as evidence.

It's as if Sirrine was a Keystone Cop who didn't realize how important the evidence was, how he was tasked to be careful with it and store it in the same condition as when he received it.

Today, the gun and its unfired cartridges would be thrown out as tainted evidence. The "expert" testing would not be allowed. "Captain" Sirrine would be significantly discredited and might even be held in contempt of court for his mishandling. At this point, the state's criminal case would teeter on the edge of dismissal.

ITEM NO. 3

The Shot in the Dark

You've heard Fred True say that he gave the gun to Archie with four bullets and got the gun back from Kate a few weeks later with only three. This was confirmed by several witnesses, Sirrine's ineptitude in handling it notwithstanding.

You've also heard Fred True and his brother Harry testify that Archie told them on the morning after he had tea with McMillan that he (Archie) had fired the gun at an alligator the night before or in the early hours that morning.

Given that a man was murdered at about this same time, possibly with the same gun, Archie's statement about firing a shot is at least curious, if not highly suspicious.

The logical question you should be asking yourself is whether anyone heard a shot ring out in the night from somewhere near the Newton house. And the answer would be yes.

A man named James A. Green lived on Crystal Lake in September 1882. He was a boarder at a house owned by Jim Rowan, which fronted the very lake where Sam's body would be discovered a few weeks later.

Green testified that on the evening of September 30, he was out in the yard about one hundred feet from the water's edge. Sometime between 9:00 and 11:00 p.m., he heard the crack of a gunshot echo in the night "distinctly and clearly." It came from the north/northwest of his location, which is the general direction of the Newton house. According to Green, the night "was clear and tolerably calm" with "just enough air stirring to move the leaves"

About thirty minutes after Green heard this gunshot, he was sitting on the porch smoking. He heard low voices out on the lake and saw, in the dim moonlight, a boat slowly gliding across the lake moving west to east. He thought it was about two hundred yards or so away from him, but he couldn't really make out any details regarding who was in the boat or how many there were.

Green assumed the people in the boat were black but had no real basis for such a belief other than the fact that the boat rowed past and into the eastern side of Lake Como, where the black cabins were located, and near the dock by the railroad tracks that was used most often by black laborers in the area.

He didn't think much of the incident until he heard some men talking a week later about Sam McMillan being missing since September 30, last seen near the Newton place. Green told the men that he heard a gunshot the night of September 30 and said, "If he had disappeared at that place that night, I heard the gun that done it."

If believed, Green's testimony tells us two main things: that a gunshot was heard from the general direction of the Newton home at about the time Sam McMillan was supposed to be leaving, and that a rowboat was seen (and heard) on the lake a short time later.

The boat could have been a pure coincidence, unrelated to Archie or Sam or anything regarding the murder. Since it seems that it proceeded to a point in the lake opposite to where the body was found and quite a ways from Newton's house, it was probably happenstance. Or the product of an active imagination.

It also may have been a misrememberance, since Green didn't mention the gunshot to anyone until one week later when a group of men were talking about Sam being missing. Green recollected the shot in the night and calculated that he had heard it on the same Saturday night one week prior.

But the boat did come from the western side of the Lake Como/Crystal Lake area, which was the area where Sam's body was discovered on October 17. If Green's story is credible, it's possible he heard the shot that killed Sam McMillan and some time later saw the murderers rowing back across the lake after dumping Sam's body on the far western side.

Unfortunately, whether Green remembered the date incorrectly or whether he even heard a gunshot on the night Sam McMillan was murdered wasn't explored by Abrams or Foster any further. This was an important piece of evidence that was introduced, emphasized for the jury (and dramatic effect), then set aside.

Add to this the fact that the search of Newton's home after October 17 by Harrison and a multitude of others (most not officially) apparently turned up nothing suspicious to indicate that a shooting had occurred anywhere inside the house. Neither lawyer introduced any evidence or asked any questions about bloodstains, clean floors, carpeting having recently been removed or the like. As such, if Archie or Kate shot Sam, it was most likely done outside, lending credibility to Green's testimony about hearing a clear gunshot in the night.

ITEM NO. 4

The Pot of Nails

According to several witnesses, when Sam's body was hauled ashore and Tony Fox cut open the bag which served as a weight, Archie Newton said "God, that's my pot." Orange grove laborer A. Pichard testified that he had seen the same pot at Newton's prior to that time, and Archie later told Fred True that the large iron pot was his; it apparently had contained paint at one time and was later used for general storage.

It was now full of nails to further weigh down the body. Several witnesses said they saw a pile of similar nails at Archie's house, in a corner either by or under the edge of the house. Some of the men saw them before Sam's disappearance, some after. Coroner Edgar Harrison added that he saw what looked like a man's finger marks in the dirt around the pile of nails, as if someone had recently been scooping them up.

A man named Joseph James was called by Prosecutor Abrams to further verify the existence of these nails. James said he was invited to play cards at Newton's "for fun" about two months before Sam disappeared. When he was there, he noticed and commented to Archie about the large pile of nails under the room next to the kitchen. They were in the soft sand on the ground and apparently constituted a large enough pile to be either unusual or remarkable enough to notice and comment on.

James wasn't asked many other questions and wasn't allowed to testify to comments made when Archie wasn't present. Not one to miss an opportunity for theatrics, however, Abrams had the actual pot—filled with the very same nails—in the courtroom for use as a prop as he talked and the story unfolded. Recording the drama for posterity, the court reporter made the following entry in the record as James stepped down from the witness stand: "Mr. Abrams here emptied the pot of nails into a newspaper to which Mr. Foster objected after same was done."

There was no expert or other examination of the pot to identify the manufacturer, a production date or other identifying characteristics. It seems as if everyone simply accepted that it was Archie's based solely on his exclamation, "God, that's my pot."

Similarly, even though they appeared to be a standard type that was available at any hardware or other dry goods store, the nails were simply accepted as Archie's. None of the several witnesses who testified about seeing the nails at Newton's house mentioned any unique or specific characteristics about the nails (color, size, type, purpose). Neither lawyer used any experts to inspect or examine the nails, and nothing was done to actually connect the nails in the pot to the pile of nails (or the keg of nails that Pichard mentioned) at the Newton property.

And of course William Sirrine's method of storing the pot and nails until trial is questionable. He testified that the nails, rope and pot were initially kept at Dodd's general store in Sanford in a "private room." But the room was not secured with a lock and key; rather, some boxes were stacked in front of or near the door, making it difficult to enter the room, which Sirrine apparently thought was adequate security. He admitted that for a few months, anyone could have entered the room and tampered with the items. He later realized this shortcoming and moved them from the store to a closet in his house. He also failed to identify them with a mark, so when produced at trial, he couldn't be 100 percent certain they were the same items given into his custody after the inquest.

The coroner, the constable, the lawyers and all the witnesses simply concluded that the pot and its nails were Archie's, without any further tests or actual identification.

ITEM NO. 5

The Rope

The pot of nails intended to weigh Sam's body down in the lake was tied around his waist with a rope. By all initial appearances, the rope was nondescript, a standard, ordinary everyday rope used by people everywhere on the frontier.

Except this one was not.

Pichard immediately recognized it as a length of rope Archie had given him a week or two before Sam's disappearance:

Q: When did you next see this rope afterwards?
A: In that place when we have the body of McMillan on the shore.

Q: Did you see that rope tied around the body of McMillan?
A: Yes, directly after the body was on the shore, Mr. Newton recognized the pot and as I was looking there at the same time my eyes struck on that knot

and directly I knew the knot and gave notice to somebody I was knowing the rope.

Q: You saw the rope around the body of the dead man?
A: Yes, around the body of the dead man.

In the spring and summer months of 1882, Pichard had been regularly working at Newton's grove. He often brought his dog with him to keep him company throughout the day.

He explained that on one occasion, a week or two before McMillan's disappearance, his dog got into a fight with the Newtons' dog. Pichard's actual words were: "Mrs. Newton and Mr. Newton make that slut fight with their dog." It's uncertain whether Pichard's French-to-English translation was unclear or whether Kate and Archie actually intentionally caused the dogs to fight. Neither lawyer followed up on this point.

But Pichard "was not pleased with that and I beat my dog one day and I put my handkerchief to her neck to carry her home." Archie saw this, went to his stable and came back with a rope for Pichard to use to walk the dog home.

The rope he gave Pichard had one knot already tied in it. Pichard thought it was "peculiar" because of the way it was tied and said at trial that it was "turned around one line and the other." It was not the standard knot used by farmers or for plowing; Pichard had done enough of both in his life and said that he could recognize different types of knots because of his experience.

Since the rope was rather smooth, he doubled it up and tied a second knot himself to get a better grip. He recognized the method he had used and the placement on the rope. Although it was starting to untie or loosen a little bit from being submerged in water for a lengthy time, he recognized it.

Pichard said he walked the dog home with the rope without further incident. He returned the rope to Newton the following Monday by placing it in a keg of nails that was on the piazza of the house. This was where he regularly put his water bucket each day, and it was visible to the household, a logical place to return the rope. He didn't see it again until October 17—tied around Sam's decomposing body.

While there is no indication that Archie ever admitted that the rope was his, the very specific and, by all accounts, credible testimony of Pichard indicate that it was. The specificity with which he identified the knot that was already present on the rope Archie handed him and his identification of the knot he (Pichard) added, combined with the context of the rope being loaned to him for his dog, makes a pretty compelling story.

One final note about Pichard, who already has shown himself to be quite a fascinating character. Foster cross-examined him extensively about the rope, the knots, where he put it and when he last saw it. But as many lawyers do when faced with a witness who gives very factual, believable testimony, he attacked the man's credibility. This he did by trying to delve into the man's political past:

Q: Where did you come from to Florida?
A: Before I went to Tallahassee? A gentleman was asking me the other day. I was in New York.

Q: Did you come to New York from France?
A: Yes.

Q: Did you leave France on account of your communistic views?
Objection that the witness political views could not be brought in to impeach him

By the Court; You may impeach his testimony but I don't think his political views in France has anything to do with his testimony.

Foster moved on to a few additional questions about the rope and the keg of nails, then finished. Pichard was dismissed, but before leaving the witness stand, he felt compelled to clarify his political views anyway, despite the fact that he didn't have to:

The witness here stated that he desired to say: that in conversation, I will say I am not a communist, I am a communer. There is a great difference between a government of the commune by itself, and not by a head. I am not a communist, I fight against it.

Perhaps he wanted to further explain because he didn't want his friends and neighbors to think he really was a communist or a political radical. This was either a reputational concern in the small, tight-knit community where he lived or was a personal safety concern as a foreigner who undoubtedly knew about frontier justice. After all, the man on trial for his life was also a foreigner who spoke with a pronounced accent, held different political views and was hoping for justice.

ITEM NO. 6

The Clothes and Jewelry

Several items of clothing were introduced at trial as part of the state's case. Some belonged to the victim, some to the accused.

To hammer home the violent nature of the murder and the macabre way the body was weighed down in the lake, Abrams introduced the actual clothing removed from McMillan's body when it was found. He showed Sam's pants, shirt, undershirt, coat and shoes to the jury. But they hadn't been cleaned and had been kept in storage for some eight months with no climate control or other treatment; they must have been quite moldy and rotten by the time Abrams paraded them about the courtroom and handed them to the jurors to pass around.

He asked Constable Sirrine to identify the shirt as the one he removed from the body on October 17 at the shore of Newton's place. Rummaging through the pile of clothing on the prosecutor's table, Abrams wanted to ask about the undershirt as well but couldn't find it and had to ask Sirrine where it was. "I have got that locked up." Everyone had to wait while he left the stand, left the courtroom and returned with the undershirt. Why he hadn't brought it or already given it to Abrams is not explained (other than by general ineptitude).

Abrams used several other witnesses to identify Sam's coat (Sirrine and Saint recognized the canvas coat with leather trim as the one they saw Sam wear often), the pants (wool with a large "bar" across the waist) and the shoes (which neighbor William Hawkins identified as those he bought for Sam to pay a bet he had lost).

Abrams also showed the jury the Stowe's Almanac that had been found inside the coat and a "postal card" addressed to McMillan.

Keeping with the horrendous nature of the murder, Abrams also had Constable Sirrine testify that one of the shoes had been recovered with part of the dead man's detached foot inside.

And as if this wasn't dramatic enough, a new piece of evidence was discovered *during* the trial. The court record notes, "Letter addressed to Samuel McMillan, postmarked August 9th and just found by the Clerk of Court in one of the pockets of the coat was offered in evidence."

The court reporter's rather casual entry belies what must have been quite a disruptive moment during the trial. Finding a letter—addressed to the murder victim—*during* the trial is practically unheard of. Not previously finding the letter despite what must have been examinations by several law enforcement officers (Coroner Harrison, Constable Sirrine, Sheriff Shine) and the prosecutor himself is inexcusable.

In addition to the dead man's rotten clothing, you'll recall that Edgar Harrison found and took as evidence several items of clothes when he executed the search warrant at the Newton house on October 20.

He testified that he found a pair of men's pants hanging in the Newtons' bedroom that appeared to be torn and dirty. Archie's clothing store friend R.L. Travis confirmed that he also saw the pants hanging in the bedroom, since he recognized it as a pair he had previously sold to Archie. Harrison also found a "ladies dress" that was soiled and had what he thought could have been "rust stains" on the front. But no further questions were asked about the dress or its condition since Kate was not on trial, and Abrams was not permitted to delve into a conspiracy theory to implicate Archie.

Harrison also found a vest in a bureau drawer in the Newtons' bedroom. The vest wasn't described at trial but it was confirmed to be Archie's. More importantly, in the right front pocket of the vest was a plain, eighteen-karat gold man's ring. There were whispers by friends and neighbors that this was the same ring that Sam owned and often wore.

We know that Sam McMillan didn't spend his money on luxury goods or amenities. By all accounts, he was a miser who lived a rather Spartan existence despite his hoard of cash and valuable orange-growing operation.

But he apparently liked jewelry and did own several conspicuous pieces, including a plain heavy gold ring. He liked to wear it to church and on special occasions and usually wore it when visiting peoples' houses or attending tea. It's for this latter reason that he likely wore it when he went to Newton's house on September 30.

Abrams felt that same way and set out to match the ring to the one found in Archie's vest pocket. He brought in J.K. Pickett, a jeweler from Salem, Ohio, who had known Sam McMillan since he was a boy. Pickett testified that he had sold a "plain" eighteen-karat gold ring and a cluster breastpin to Sam in 1876. Pickett said that he was in Sam's "debt a little," so he sold the ring at a lower price than normal to help settle up their accounts.

He last saw the ring in 1880, when Sam was back in Salem for a visit and asked Pickett to clean it and buff out some of the scratches.

Abrams held up the ring found in the front pocket of the vest belonging to Archie Newton and said, "State whether or not that ring looks anything like the ring you sold to Samuel McMillan?"

Pickett examined the ring on the witness stand, and initially said with confidence, "[T]hat looks very much indeed like the ring." But as he looked further, he commented that the ring was scratched, quite worn and "soiled."

Looking at the inside of the gold band, Pickett then said he could not find any evidence of the private mark he engraved for identification purposes onto all jewelry he sold. In fact, he couldn't find evidence of any marks, other than the "18-kt" stamp.

Abrams asked a series of questions suggesting that the scratches and wear inside the ring might have been intentional, as if someone was trying to rub out the mark so the ring could not be identified. Pickett agreed that it could have been intentional, that wearing the finish of the ring like that would not be likely from normal wearing. But he also noted that continuous wear by someone "working in dirt or sand" may also cause similar wear.

When asked definitively by Foster on cross-examination to swear that it was the ring he sold to McMillan, Picket could only respond, "I am willing to swear it looks like it."

> *Q: That isn't it?*
> *A: As I have failed to find my private mark in there I should hate to swear it was the ring I sold him.*

It's also interesting to note that Pickett said that he had ridden the train to Florida with David McMillan, Sam's brother. They both journeyed from Ohio for the trial. Foster asked if he had discussed the ring with David McMillan while on that long trip, clearly expecting Pickett to reply in the affirmative. Foster perhaps wanted to raise some question as to Pickett's credibility or sympathies or even motive for testifying.

But curiously, Pickett said that he did not speak to David about the ring as they journeyed to Florida. We can picture Foster being taken aback slightly at this answer, and although he didn't really question Pickett further about it, this response may have called his credibility into question.

Abrams also called H. Lord to the stand, a jeweler in Sanford who had sold Archie several items after Sam disappeared. Lord said that on October 4, 1882, Archie bought a small silver hunting watch, a gold fluted chain and a gold-filled ring. He paid cash, although Lord didn't notice anything remarkable about the greenbacks.

Abrams again held up the ring found in Archie's vest pocket and said, "Was that the ring you sold to Mr. Newton?" Lord was certain it was not the same ring. Abrams therefore tried twice, with two different witnesses, to establish that the ring they did find in Archie's possession was actually Sam's, but failed. He was left only with the inference that it was.

Lord also noted that a year or so before, he had sold Archie some alligator teeth jewelry and "fish scale jewelry." These were some of the items Archie sent to Kate while she still lived in London and confirm Mrs. Jones's statements about their relationship in 1880–81.

ITEM NO. 7

Bromidia

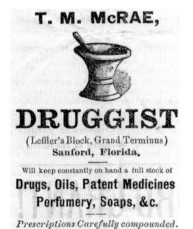

T. M. McRAE,

DRUGGIST

(Leffler's Block, Grand Terminus)
Sanford, Florida.

Will keep constantly on hand a full stock of

Drugs, Oils, Patent Medicines
Perfumery, Soaps, &c.

Prescriptions Carefully compounded.
Dec. 21st, 1882-tf.

Advertisement for druggist T.M. McRae, who sold Archie Newton two heavy doses of sleeping drugs on two consecutive days in 1882. *Sanford Museum Collection.*

We've seen that while still in London, Archie Newton was accused of inappropriate behavior by Pollie Bowron, Kate's sister. This certainly included a sexual encounter that allegedly made her pregnant. But it may also have included something far more sinister than seduction: it might have included the use of a sleeping drug to take advantage of her. This twist on the story of Archie's time in London with the Bowron sisters was suggested by one newspaper article reporting on Archie's murder trial as it unfolded. But this fact was not proven, and the reporter didn't cite any specific source.

But it's worth mentioning here because we know that Archie Newton bought sleeping powder during his time in Sanford, Florida. And he apparently knew how to use it.

Sometime during the morning of October 1, 1882, the day after McMillan's disappearance and at some point after he had visited Pichard, Zeri Adams, Emile Tissot and Fred True, Archie stopped into the drugstore of T.M. McRae in downtown Sanford. He told the druggist that he wanted something to "quiet the nerves and produce sleep."

McRae apparently didn't think too much of it and gave him one ounce of "Bromidia." This was an especially powerful drug, as McRae explained:

> *In prescriptions it is not intended for general use, it is only prescribed by physicians for use as an anodyne. Physicians only are intended to use it: it is not generally meant to go out among the people. They only use it to quiet the nervous system and use it in persons where there is considerable nervous excitement but as a* [rule] *they give it more to produce sleep. There is* [sic] *no narcotic principles about it, nothing like opium, only to quiet the nervous system.*

Ads for bromidia described it as a true "hypnotic" with an ingredient list that includes chloral hydrate, bromide of potassium and cannabis extract. As McRae said, it wasn't as strong as opium but was nonetheless a strong sleeping agent.

According to McRae, Archie said that it was for his wife. He gave no other explanation, and McRae didn't ask for any. The ounce he gave Archie would provide eight individual doses of one teaspoonful each.

By itself, this purchase isn't especially unusual. Bad nerves or "nervous excitement" were common diagnoses in the late nineteenth century by both doctors and laypersons alike. Opium was still in use, but its addictive effects made it less popular as the century wore on.

But Archie's purchase of a powerful sleeping drug was not done in a vacuum. It comes in the context of his possibly having used it two years before to take advantage of Kate's sister. And it comes in the context of the fact that he may just have killed a man a few hours before, and both he and Kate were incredibly nervous and stressed about it and might not have slept for twenty-four-plus hours.

Also keep in mind that Archie stopped by Pichard's house on Sunday morning and asked Mrs. Pichard for a bottle of wine. He indicated that he hadn't slept well.

The suspicious nature of the bromidia purchase is compounded by the fact that it wasn't the only one. Archie came back to McRae's *the very next day* and asked for more.

McRae didn't inquire as to why he needed more or whether Archie had actually used the entire first bottle up in one day (which would have been most inadvisable from a medical standpoint). He simply made another batch. (He couldn't recall if he gave him the powerful Bromidia again, or made a "bromide of potash" compound of his own mixing.) Either way,

Archie Newton bought two large doses of a powerful sleeping drug on two separate occasions within twenty-four hours.

At this point, the trial was going on four weeks. The Thursday, June 28, 1883 edition of the *Sanford Journal* suggested that the end was approaching:

> *"Local Intelligence"*
> *Mr. Lever, Foreman, having just returned from Orlando where he had been called to testify in the Newton case, informs us that it is expected the testimony for the State will close this week. It is thought the end of the case will be reached by the last of next week.*

> *"Sylvan Lake Items"*
> *Most of the men of this neighborhood are residing at Orlando for the present, witnesses in the Newton case. Our butcher is there too, and now it is bacon or none.*

ITEM NO. 8

King Wylly's Medical Opinion

The prosecution's star witness was Dr. King Wylly, a local physician who had served as a surgeon for the Confederate army in the Civil War and the French army in the Franco-Prussian War.

He examined McMillan's body a short time after it was pulled from the lake and gave a graphic description of its condition. He opined that the body had been placed in the water at least thirty to sixty minutes after death and not any sooner. He dated the death (based on the state of decomposition) at ten to fourteen days prior to its discovery. He noted that the "broken tissue showed that fish, turtles or something had eaten it and perhaps the motion of the waves had caused the different joints to give way and fall off."

Foster asked him on cross-examination whether there was any sign the body had been "otherwise disposed of before it was put into the water." Wylly responded that he "couldn't say" and that he had "no opinion" on that possibility because there was no evidence of it: "There was nothing on which I can base an opinion. I saw nothing whatever."

Dr. King Wylly. *Sanford
Museum Collection.*

When Abrams asked if there were "any marks of violence on the body,"
Wylly said:

> *The detachment of the collarbone, and the left first rib from the breast bone
> might have been caused by violence. The condition of the body was such that
> I could not judge. I think it might have been but I could not assert it as a fact.*

When asked if there were any marks or abrasions on the body that would
suggest violence, Wylly said:

> *I could not state now. I thought then there was, but I have since looked well
> into the matter and the time between the death of McMillan and the finding
> of the body was so great, I would not risk any opinion.*

Abrams tried a few more times in a few different ways, but Dr. Wylly
was very clear that he could not say for certain that any physical violence

was committed on Sam's body. That undercut several of the points of the indictment against Archie and left the gunshot as the sole crime.

Dr. Wylly also examined the head, but only in a cursory fashion. He was not present at the October 21 exam where Dr. Caldwell scraped the brain material out with a metal wire and shook the bullet out. Rather, Wylly saw the skull later and not with an eye toward testifying about it. He only noticed the hole in the lower back portion of the cranium and, even though his exam was brief, provided a much better medical evaluation than Dr. Caldwell:

Q: Can you state as a medical opinion what caused that hole?
A: Well, I should presume that a bullet had made the hole, a projectile of some kind.

Q: Would a projectile of any kind passing through that or into be likely to cause death?

Objection that witness did not notice it with a view of testifying, therefore he could not swear as to it.

By the Court: He may state as a physician, what his knowledge is, or what would be the result of that.

To which ruling of the court counsel for the defense then and there excepted.

A: I had better state where the hole was.

Q: State all that?
A: There was a hole.

Objection that the head was not identified as being the head of Samuel McMillan.

By the Court: I know that. I don't know what the testimony hereinafter may disclose.

Q: Go on?
A: The hole in the head was made to the right of the occipital ridge.

Q: State in plain English doctor where the hole was?
A: That is the vertical ridge that goes from the back of the head down the center of the neck. This projectile struck the edge of the ridge and evidently turned and entered on the right of the ridge and entered the cavity of the skull. I noticed the ridge split—the fragment of bone evidently went in with the projectile. That's all I noticed.

Q: I ask you as an expert what would be the character of a wound from a projectile entering the back of the head in the manner testified to by you?
A: That would produce instant death.

Q: Then such a wound would be mortal?
A: Yes.

As noted, Wylly was a veteran battlefield doctor who had served in two wars on two continents. He was more than qualified to speak of bullet wounds and their effects on the human body, and his summary of the path of the bullet that entered Sam's head was the most detailed of the entire case.

As to the head being detached from the body, Wylly was asked only one question as to how this came to be:

Q: Should you say from the appearance of the vertebrae that the head was separated from the body by decomposition, the action of the water?
A: It might have occurred that way.

Despite the prosecution's implications, there was no conclusive evidence that Sam had been beheaded after or as part of his death. Even though Abrams elicited the testimony about Archie looking to borrow a razor on the morning after the murder, and even though he suggested that this might have been for beheading, there was no proof. And neither of the doctors who examined the head and the body was able to conclude that it had been removed by the murderer.

This is supported by two simple facts: a shaving razor would have been the least efficient and perhaps most difficult method of removing a human head. Archie's behavior in asking to borrow a razor the day after Sam's disappearance was certainly odd, as we've seen, and his explanation about wanting to be clean-shaven because he and Kate expected company later that day was not borne out by events. But the use of an axe or hatchet would have been much more expedient to render a body headless, and Archie had plenty of those available at his own house.

Second, almost every lake or standing body of water in Florida contains alligators. Many contain large snapping turtles, and all contain many species of fish large and small. Alligator populations were greater in 1882 than today, and a submerged human body would have been easy feeding for all manner of lake creatures.

Further, when found on October 21, Sam McMillan's detached head was not weighted down as the body had been. And it was located only twenty-five feet or so from the body. There really wasn't any reason for the killer to decapitate the body, leave all identifying information on it but then casually discard the head nearby where it was easily discoverable. It's therefore most likely that Sam's head was removed not by the murderer but by any of the number of creatures that inhabit Florida's lakes.

Dr. King Wylly performed one other examination that yielded critical information in this case. Edgar Harrison had found and removed two handkerchiefs from Newton's room when he searched the house on October 19. The edges of those handkerchiefs were spotted with what Harrison thought was rust or perhaps blood.

At trial, Abrams established the authenticity of the handkerchiefs by handing them dramatically to Constable Sirrine and asking, "State where you received those things?" Sirrine said he was given them by Harrison, and they were in his possession until taken for "microscopic examination."

Dr. Wylly performed that "microscopic examination" in October by examining the larger of the two handkerchiefs and taking a sample from one corner that contained a reddish spot. Under the microscope, he said the spot proved to contain "iron pigment," showing itself to be rust or metallic in origin. Since Newton owned tools and worked in cultivating trees and the handkerchief appeared to be his, this finding was not unusual.

But Wylly also found what he called "one blood crystal" on the handkerchief section during his examination. However, he found no others in the sample he took and ultimately concluded that he had scratched his own hand or finger with a fingernail and caused the presence of the blood crystal: "[W]e gave the doubt to the prisoner and decided it was not blood."

He also noted that when examining the handkerchief, it looked to have been recently washed because it "looked clean and fresh" and had no other dirt or marks on it other than the rust-stained edges. He theorized that it had been washed recently with soda and water but could not be sure. He could only be sure of those iron pigment rust spots and one blood crystal staining the edge.

Based on the findings of his first examination, he testified at the preliminary hearing in October 1882 that there was no blood present on the handkerchiefs.

But by the time of the trial in June 1883, the handkerchiefs presented to the jury by Prosecutor Abrams looked entirely different. When Abrams held them up and handed them to Wylly, the doctor said: "I can state that the handkerchiefs don't look as it did when we had it under examination before. I think these tinges have come out since. That iron rust was there, but these other colors have appeared since."

The handkerchiefs produced at trial in June 1883 were no longer clean white with some stained edges; they were now covered with multiple reddish spots and areas of discoloration. It looked like a magician's cheap parlor trick had been performed in the months since Harrison confiscated them from Archie's room and Wylly first examined them.

But Dr. Wylly deftly explained this magic away with science:

> *Q: State whether or not* [the spots] *could have been there at the time and not been apparent?*
> *A: Yes.*
>
> *Q: Explain to the jury why?*
> *A: Washing with soda would have taken the coloring out of the red corpuscles of the blood.*
>
> *Q: Then why reappear?*
> *A: The coloring matter of the blood will absorb oxygen and reappear.*

It must have strained the jury's credulity to hear that in October, the handkerchiefs were white and clean with a few rust stains on the edges and nothing else. The initial expert microscopic examination found no evidence of any blood. But now eight months later in June, both handkerchiefs contained multiple visible spots and "tinges" of red just in time for a murder trial.

But Dr. Wylly's description of oxygen absorption was acceptable to the state of science in 1883. Abrams, of course, was satisfied with this explanation. Foster did not cross-examine Wylly on this point and did not present any experts to counter this theory or the doctor's findings. Judge

Cocke asked no questions about it from the bench, and the jurors were left to ponder.

Wylly went on to explain that he re-tested the red-stained handkerchiefs approximately one week prior to his testimony and, not surprisingly, found something quite different.

On his second go-round with the handkerchiefs, he cut a small piece from the center of one of the larger red spots, put it on a glass slide and added a few drops of water. He examined the specimen by holding it with one needle and "picking at it" with another. In this way, he found "blood corpuscles, capillaries" that resembled the basic structures of blood. He couldn't tell whether it came from an artery or vein because the cell bodies he viewed were not sufficient to make that determination. But they were sufficient to conclude that they were blood cells with the attendant structural characteristics well known to medical science.

Notably absent from his findings was the presence of any brain tissue or other evidence of trauma to the human head. Since Sam had been shot in the back of the head at close range, and if the handkerchief was exposed to the blood spatter or used to wipe the resulting mess, one would expect at least some indication of brain tissue in these spots. But there weren't any, and nothing suggested where the blood came from.

While defense attorney Foster was cross-examining Dr. Wylly about this crucial piece of evidence, Abrams interrupted and said, "I desire here to say that it is a matter well known to medical science that brain tissue disappears in a few minutes." Foster paused and replied sarcastically, "[W] ell Dr. Abrams." Abrams smugly explained in reply that he was the son of a doctor and proud of his own medical knowledge. Foster turned to Judge Cocke and said:

> *Dr. Abrams was not on the stand, was not cross-examined, and has no right to argue notorious facts as he says, but if I am to be interrupted, whenever I discuss these experts, and show their inconsistency, why, I will simply state what Dr. Wylly says, and let him and Dr. Abrams talk it out.*

The court reporter didn't note whether there was laughter in the courtroom at this back-and-forth, but we can imagine the reaction at Abrams's histrionics and Foster's sarcastic retorts. The record does contain several subsequent pages of detailed medical explanation and description of corpuscles, capillaries, anamosis and tessalation from Dr. Wylly. He explained at length how such blood may have ended up on the cloth. Because of the structure of the blood ("There were epithelial scales of the tessalated variety"), he concluded that it resulted from a wound that was not neat and clean but rather "a wound that is torn when the tissue is destroyed." It wasn't the type of blood found in a regular cut on the hand or a nose bleed, and it wasn't menstrual blood. Quite emphatically, he opined, "It was blood from a torn wound." This conclusion begged the obvious question: why would Archie possess two handkerchiefs that had spots of blood spatter all over their surfaces? And the fact that he had vigorously scrubbed both to a snowy white only made him seem guiltier.

However, despite all the big words and medical theory and blood-red spots, Dr. Wylly could not answer the most important question of all on cross-examination:

> *Q: Can you swear these blood corpuscles are human blood?*
> *A: No.*
>
> *Q: Whatever they were, can you swear they came from a living person or a dead person?*
> *A: No.*

Foster didn't ask any more questions about human blood and probably missed a solid line of inquiry about food (Could the blood have come from wiping your hands while eating meat?) or pets (Could the blood have come from the Newtons' dog or a raccoon Archie trapped or a fish he caught and cleaned?).

He also didn't ask the simple question of whether this was Archie's own blood. He had, after all, borrowed a straight razor on October 1 to shave with; wasn't it plausible that he used his handkerchief to wipe his face at some point afterward?

Foster missed these points, perhaps because the good doctor was not done. This most recent test of the now-spotted handkerchiefs also revealed one more explosive piece of evidence: a single piece of coarse red hair.

It was barely visible to the naked eye, measuring only one-twentieth of an inch. Wylly explained it was seen "only if your attention was called to it with a microscope." He said he found it in the sample he took from the center of one of the larger red spots, which led him to conclude it was part of whatever caused the spatter.

Since it was not visible to the eye, he determined the color of the microscopic piece of hair by examining its "prismatic rays of light." When tested this way, it showed that "red was the predominating color. It paled one way into blue, and then into orange yellow, and finally a tinge of green." This test result showed that the single hair was red. The courtroom must have been breathless at this revelation, since everyone knew that Sam McMillan had red hair.

It's therefore an understatement to say that the existence of a single piece of red hair—in the middle of a stain that may have been human blood—on the handkerchief of the accused murderer was powerful. It raised multiple obvious and damning questions about Archie Newton, who must have slumped at the defendant's table as Wylly pronounced his expert opinions from the witness stand.

Foster didn't give up, though, and tried hard to cast doubt on the obvious conclusions that flowed from this revelation:

Q: Couldn't that piece of hair, small as it was, have got into that handkerchief during it's wearing?
A: Oh yes. I don't know how it got there.

Q: It may have come from the person wearing it?
A: I don't know.

Q: You don't know how it got there, you simply testify you found such a thing?
A: Yes.

But Abrams skillfully got Wylly to agree that the red hair could have come from a "fracture or wound in the skull just as readily as being woven into the handkerchief."

After Dr. Wylly sent the courtroom buzzing, Abrams called Sam's neighbor J.O. Tabor back to the stand to confirm that Sam had indeed been a redhead. He agreed that Sam's hair was "a reddish color" and that his beard had been "sandy red." Foster promptly stood and asked one question, trying hard to fight the conclusion that Archie was a murderer:

Q: By reddish how did it compare with Mr. Saint's hair—for instance? Do you mean the same sort of color?
A: Similar.

Not to be outdone on this point, Abrams felt compelled to recall Charles Saint himself, the Twin Lakes neighbor to whom Foster had just referred:

Q: What was the color of Samuel McMillan's hair?
A: It was what they call red I believe.

Q: Was it anything like any hair you have noticed?
A: Why yes. I don't believe mine is red but it was something between this (beard) *and this* (hair of the head).

With this curious ending (and a completely different and unexplored line of inquiry, I think, about whether the red hair was that of Charles Saint or someone other than Sam McMillan), the state rested its case. It was July 3, 1883.

VERDICT

After Dr. Wylly's medical testimony and the brief questions to Tabor and Saint about red hair, the court took a recess until 9:00 a.m. on July 5. Judge Cocke then came back and announced a recess until July 5 at noon "for cause shown" to allow defense time "to announce" whether and what witnesses it would put on.

The July 5, 1883 edition of the *Sanford Journal* contained the following summary about the recent developments:

The Newton Trial
We are informed that on yesterday [Monday] *the State "rested" in the presentation of the Newton case. It is not known to us at this writing whether or not the defense will introduce any testimony. We learn that during the last few days, the prosecution has gotten in some very damaging testimony against the accused. A portion derived from a witness who has lately arrived from England, and a portion from experts, who have discovered certain stains on handkerchiefs found in the possession, or in the house of, the accused, to be blood stains. It is possible that before going to press, we may learn the course of the defense.*

Foster ultimately informed the court that Archie Newton would not be testifying on his own behalf and that the defense would not put on any witnesses or introduce any evidence. This was a strategic move by Foster and one that defense lawyers sometimes make when they either don't have any good evidence to introduce or they think their cross-examination of the prosecution witnesses was sufficiently damaging. Foster may also have wanted to convey to the jury his feeling that the defense was so strong and evidence so weak that his client couldn't possibly be convicted.

Two days of closing arguments ensued, and Judge Cocke finally read the jury its instructions about the law and its duties on Saturday, July 7. They left the courtroom at 10:00 a.m., and everyone waited.

The weather in early July had been "intensely hot," as described by one of the trial attendees. It was ninety-eight to ninety-nine degrees day in and day out, with little to no rain, no air conditioning and little fresh air. Archie Newton, the lawyers, the court clerks and all those who packed the courtroom to watch the trial literally were sweating it out as they waited.

According to the Orange County log books, the jury came back at 3:00 p.m. and asked for further instruction. Judge Cocke gave them additional instruction (to which Foster objected) and sent them back to the deliberation room.

The jury then informed the judge at 5:00 p.m. that they had reached a verdict. Everyone was called back to the courtroom to hear the outcome. Archie must have nervously stood at the defense table with Foster as the jury filed back into the courtroom. Abrams was probably pretty confident, as was his nature, but the lack of any direct evidence—his prosecution had relied solely on a string of circumstantial and not always connected facts—was a huge question mark in a case like this.

With enough tension to make even the most hardened person nervous, the verdict was read: "We the jury find the accused Archibald W. Newton guilty as charged in the indictment."

According to newspaper accounts, there was "much excitement in the courtroom" when the verdict was read. Judge Cocke banged his gavel for order. He discharged the jury, ordered Archie to be remanded back to jail and adjourned until "Monday morning" for sentencing.

Just like that, it was over.

And sentencing was equally swift; when court reconvened a few days later on July 11, 1883, Judge Cocke read his sentence:

> *The law of this State inflicts the punishment of death on any person convicted of murder in the first degree. You have, after a full and fair trial on evidence before a Jury of your County with the assistance of able Counsel*

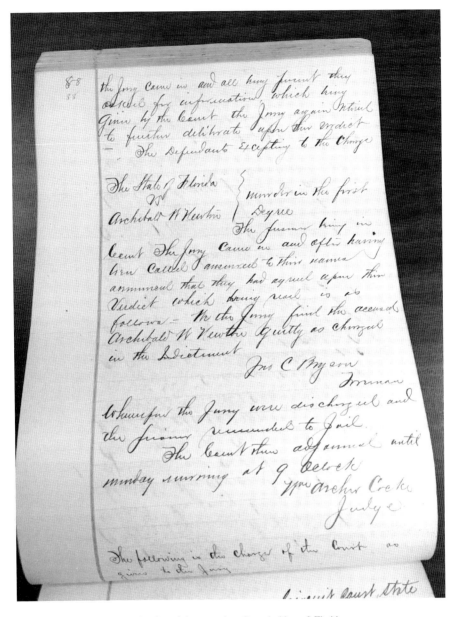

Guilty verdict as recorded in the trial transcript. *State Archives of Florida.*

Sentenced to hang. *State Archives of Florida.*

been thus convicted. It is made the duty of the Court to pass sentence on you according to law. That sentence is that the punishment of death be inflicted on you by hanging by the neck until you are dead.

Sheriff Shine was "directed to inflict such punishment on you, in the walls or enclosure of the jail of Orange County" on a date to be appointed and was further instructed to keep Archie in "close confinement" until that time.

As you may imagine, the story was salacious and widely reported all over Florida, the South and the United States. Many reporters noted that the "verdict of the jury accords with popular sentiment" regarding Archie's guilt. For the next few weeks, newspapers printed variations of the following basic article:

A Drop of Blood and a Red Hair

Archibald W. Newton, a young man who belonged to a wealthy family which stands high in England, was recently convicted in Orange County, Florida, of the murder of Samuel McMillan. The case was sensational, and when the jury brought in the verdict, "We find the prisoner guilty as charged in the indictment," there was much excitement in the court room.

In the spring of 1881 Newton appeared at Sanford, Florida. He was a youth of fine appearance and pleasing manners, and was popular at first, but his good reputation was soon blasted. There were reasons to suspect him of forgeries, and then came news that he had left England because of an outrage against Miss Polly Bowron. Subsequently he sent money to England for Kate Bowron, a sister of his alleged victim, and, meeting her in New York, married her, and the couple returned to Crystal Lake, Orange County.

While this was going on another topic of suspicion presented itself. There lived in Orange County, near Crystal Lake, a man named Samuel McMillan, who bore the reputation of being a miser, and was supposed to carry a large sum of money on his person. On Saturday evening, McMillan was seen alive half an hour after sunset in company with Newton. He never returned to his home, and about three weeks after his headless body was found in Crystal Lake, partly consumed by fish,

Around the waist was a rope, to which was suspended a sack, in which was found an iron pot full of nails. A few days later the head of the murdered man was found near the same spot, and a bullet hole was discovered in the back of his skull. On the brain being removed a bullet dropped out, it appeared to fit a pistol Newton had borrowed from a neighbor named True.

About that time Newton became flush of funds. He said that his wife's brother, James Bowron, had sent him 25,000 dollars with which to buy an orange grove on the lake. He was suspected of the murder of McMillan, however, and was brought before Judge Cooke [sic]. The sensation of the trial occurred when counsel for prosecution walked down the aisle, followed by a medium-sized, dark haired woman, evidently a foreigner. As the stranger got abreast of Mrs. Newton she turned and peered into her face, saying: "Why Kate-!" The prisoner, as he looked up and recognised the woman, flashed until it seemed the blood would burst from his neck and cheeks, while Mrs. Newton turned deathly pale and remained several seconds with upturned face and half-opened lips, as if petrified by amazement. The presence of this woman in America was a complete surprise to the defence. Her testimony was to the effect that the Bowron family had not £25 in the world, much less 25,000 dollars to invest in orange groves. That had been the main point of the defence—to account for Newton's money, alleged to have been sent by the wealthy, brother-in-law.

McMillan, the murdered man, had coarse red hair. At the trial Dr. King Wylly testified that he had found blood-spots on a handkerchief found in Newton's pocket the morning after the murder and a single red hair. He testified that at the first examination he found a single blood crystal. Supposing that he might have scratched his finger and caused the crystal to get on the handkerchief, he would not accept it as evidence that there was blood there. His last examination revealed the blood corpuscles very distinctly, and under the microscope he discovered a single red hair—a coarse red hair. The defence argued the case point by point, but the drift was against them, and when Newton said that he had borrowed True's pistol to shoot an alligator, the audience laughed.

When the jury came in and gave the verdict, one could have heard a pin drop. All the while Newton had been nervously twitching his moustache. When the verdict was read out he dropped his head and turned deathly pale, while a slight tremor passed through his frame. He then suddenly jumped up and seized his hat, forgetting that the court had not adjourned, but presently controlled himself and resumed his seat. His wife remained quiet for a few moments, then a few tears trickled down her cheeks, and she grasped her husband's arm convulsively, but beyond this she showed no emotion, while the Judge pronounced sentence of death.

The August 6, 1883 *New York Evening Post* ran an article with the headline "A Remarkable Murder Trial. Convicted by Circumstantial Evidence." On

August 11, 1883, the *Chicago Tribune* ran a piece titled "One Red Hair: How It Unraveled a Florida Mystery—Murder of a Miser."

It was reported in major newspapers in Cleveland, Atlanta, Philadelphia and San Francisco.

Given Archie's British connection, the story was carried in newspapers in London, Wales, Ireland and Scotland, often with the headline "An Anglo-American Romance of Crime" (*Ayr (Ireland) Advertiser*). It was reported as far away as Australia and the *Southland Times* in New Zealand.

Archie Newton was now notorious worldwide.

9

GETTING AWAY WITH MURDER

APPEAL

Not surprisingly, Foster immediately moved for a new trial, which was denied by Judge Cocke. Foster then advised that Archie would appeal the conviction to the Florida Supreme Court.

This had the dual effect of postponing the death sentence and forcing Abrams to spend an inordinate amount of extra time on a case he had just won. Both lawyers wrote numerous motions, briefs and filings.

The appeal also preserved the trial transcript, which is an essential part of any legal appeal even today. Appellate judges read all the pleadings and motions and briefs and reference the actual trial record as they review the legal arguments and the facts on which the trial court relied. They evaluate whether the trial judge made any legal or procedural errors and assess whether those errors unduly influenced the jury or caused other irreparable harm to the defendant.

The imposing James Ingraham, who had initially met and assisted Archie when he first arrived in Florida in November 1880, was conflicted by the conviction and felt compelled to try to do something. He wrote a detailed letter to Henry Sanford on August 8, 1883, with a plea for help on Newton's behalf:

General H.S. Sanford.
Dear Sir.

I wrote you several days ago, enclosing a copy of the Tavares Herald, *containing an account of the Newton trial. Which, while it is not altogether entirely true, will give you an idea of the points of the prosecution. As you may judge from its tone, the general feeling against him, is intense; no doubt seeming to exist of his guilt in the minds of the public. The circumstances are against him, but, we cannot think they are more than a wonderful combination of trivial circumstances. That, with the murder occurring at the time, created suspicion against him especially as he could not account for the money he spent, and deposited in bank, shortly afterwards.*

He seems perfectly strong in his conviction that the guilty party, will be found before the time comes for him to be hung. And is as cool and collected as any one else is, about him. His wife, the same.

It is very strange that his friends do not take any steps to find out if he did have any expectations from England. Or if his wife did get any money from her brother in Hull, to bring with her. She claims that she brought some $800 with her. That she saved, and was the money that they spent after the murder. Foster has written and cabled time and again, about the matter, but he gets nothing in reply, only meets with the most sublime indifference. We feel that if he is guilty that he must be punished; but as we are so sure of his innocence, it seems to us a most cruel thing that those who ought to feel an interest in people of their own blood, should be so insensible to his danger of suffering the extreme penalty of the law, when so little trouble might save his life; if his story of expectations from his wife's family be true. For the sake of common humanity won't you take some steps in his behalf.

This letter shows the proper deference to Henry Sanford's status (although Ingraham no longer worked for him), but also suggests an undertone of criticism of Sanford's failure thus far to help Archie.

It also shows that Ingraham, despite his impassive testimony at trial, stayed in contact with Foster and perhaps Archie throughout the trial and in the months after. He certainly seemed to lean toward Archie's innocence, and his practical side couldn't fathom how Kate's family was refusing to help.

The silence from Hull may have been related to the accusations leveled by her sister Pollie in 1880. Recall that Kate didn't believe Pollie and essentially accused her of lying about Archie's improper conduct, seduction and her pregnancy. What better way for Pollie to get back at the sister who didn't believe her, and probably had maligned her, than to orchestrate a wall of silence when that sister most needed help? This may suggest that the Bowron family viewed Kate's marriage to Archie and her immigration to America as unforgivable, and they refused to help her despite the murder charge.

Whatever the case, their failure to back up Archie's claim that he and Kate had received a substantial sum from England just before Sam's death created an opening that Abrams masterfully exploited. Among the other circumstantial evidence, he spent much time on the fact that Sam McMillan possessed and often carried with him large amounts of cash. He went missing and likely was killed on the evening of September 30, 1882, and the Newtons were immediately seen (as early as Monday, October 2) in Sanford spending large amounts of cash. They bought clothing, jewelry and a new buggy; they visited several stores and paid their credit balances in full with cash. Archie was seen by many friends and neighbors with a large roll of cash just after Sam's disappearance, something very atypical for the man who relied on his monthly allowance. And he inexplicably traveled to Jacksonville on October 5 and deposited a significant sum of money in a bank there.

Since all the contextual testimony pointed to the fact that the Newtons had very little money prior to this (and essentially lived paycheck-to-paycheck), the conclusion about where they suddenly got the money was rather easy to reach.

But this was all circumstance; there was no direct evidence that Archie killed Sam McMillan and took his money. Even the newspaper accounts of the trial and conviction focused on the circumstantial nature of the evidence:

> *But the evidence as well as the circumstances of the murder all pointed to Newton as the guilty party. Each link in the chain of evidence only seemed a connection between other links, and the testimony of each witness seemed to weave the web more closely about the accused. There seemed absolutely no avenue of escape.*

In fact, the earliest articles about Sam's murder questioned whether the circumstances were enough to find guilt. Reports of the coroner's inquest noted that "the facts elicited by the examination of the various witnesses, brought out a chain of circumstantial evidence." The *South Florida Journal* (Thursday, October 26, 1882) had even warned:

The wild rumors that have been floating around have been avoided. Public opinion in passing judgment should be governed by facts alone, and should be slow in forming, remembering always to give the accused parties the benefit of all doubt. It is a grave offence to be charged with, and no means should be left unemployed to prove the accused innocent, if innocent, or to fasten the guilt upon the right parties.

After reviewing all the information, including the one-thousand-page trial transcript that has told you much of this story, the Florida Supreme Court overturned the conviction. In its opinion (recorded as occurring in the June 1884 term, but likely not issued until December 1884 or early 1885), the court determined that the circumstantial evidence presented so deftly by Abrams at trial was not enough to support the guilty verdict.

Sparing you the detailed legal jargon and discussions of special venires, pleas in abatement, demurrers and extra-territorial commissions, here are the main findings of the Supreme Court in awarding a new trial:

1. The trial court did not have discretion to deny the right to interview the three witnesses that lived outside of Florida (the two employees of Winchester Repeating Arms Company and Colt Arms Manufacturing Company and Kate's brother Thomas Bowron in Hull, England); in fact, it had a <u>duty</u> to allow it. Foster had sufficiently proved that their testimony was material. Abrams's move to admit that they would testify as indicated was not sufficient because it didn't admit to the truth of what they would say. Denying the right to depose the three witnesses and forcing Archie to trial was a reversible error by Judge Cocke.

2. A personal, in-court statement made by Abrams's co-counsel Thomas Wilson about what someone told him in the hallway during the trial was not permissible and should have been prohibited. Wilson made his statement about James Cowan, who had testified earlier that day about possibly seeing Sam McMillan on the streets of Sanford in the week after his disappearance. But Cowan confirmed that it was not Sam and was someone else; he also refuted the suggestion that Archie had told Cowan it would be a "personal favor" if Cowan said it was Sam. Wilson claimed that another witness (Harry True) told him that Cowan was not being truthful. Judge Cocke had allowed Wilson's statement, but the Supreme Court said this "personal" statement had the effect of undermining the witness's own testimony.

3. The testimony of Ellen Jones (the London boardinghouse owner who knew Kate) was "immaterial and improper" and should have been prohibited. In fact, the court found that it was wholly unfounded and "incompetent" and prejudiced the jury against Newton.

4. Remarks made by Abrams in his closing argument to compare Newton's case with two other criminals who had been convicted were improper and should have been stopped by Judge Cocke.

5. Part of Judge Cocke's jury instructions—regarding an automatic finding of premeditation—was improper and also served as grounds for reversing the guilty verdict.

The Florida Supreme Court formally reversed the guilty verdict of the jury and ordered a new trial. The view of the justices about the trial is best summed by the following from their opinion:

Here, the defendant's life was at stake, the proof as to Newton was all circumstantial, nothing whatever direct—how careful then should the court be in the admission of evidence; and permit nothing that bore upon the case in the least degree to go to the jury, unless warranted by law or the rules of evidence.

It was a complete victory for Archie Newton.

RETRIAL

Unfortunately, no records regarding the second trial have been found, and it received scant mention in available newspaper articles. We do know that Archie had to wait until November 1886 to get his second chance.

By this time, E.K. Foster had been elected a judge in the same judicial circuit. He spent part of 1886 conducting the first official court sessions in a small port town in South Florida called Miami (Dade County at that time was in Foster's territory). Judge Foster was much celebrated by Miami's citizenry for travelling to and establishing regular judicial order in their growing town.

Abrams's tenure as prosecutor ended in 1884, and he was deeply involved with the building of Tavares, Florida, the town about thirty miles west of

Sanford he had founded in 1880. In fact, he spent much of his time in a bitter fight to get the state capital moved to his tiny town in the middle of nowhere, frustrated at his own lack of political muscle (or, more likely, miscalculating the influence he actually had).

While awaiting his new trial, Archie appears in the 1885 Florida State Census (recorded June 30, 1885) as "prisoner in jail." This was a new facility, built in 1884 for a whopping $10,000. It was bigger and probably was an improvement for what may have been its longest-tenured inmate. It had been built in response to the increase in crime that resulted from the approval (in 1883) of liquor sales in Orange County.

By the time the retrial rolled around in 1886, most of the key witnesses had either moved away, died or their memories weren't as sharp about events from the fall of 1882. Sam McMillan was still mourned, but there was no McMillan connection left in Sanford: his property had been sold at an estate auction and no family members ever came back to Florida. The frontier was growing and changing, and people had moved on.

Moreover, as noted in the Florida Supreme Court's opinion, several key aspects of the state's case were now prohibited. Ellen Jones was not permitted to help establish Archie and Kate's lack of money; the cost of taking now required depositions outside the state was significant; and the lawyers had changed.

Given these developments, Archie Newton was found not guilty in the first week of December 1886 and acquitted of all charges in the death of Samuel McMillan.

He was finally a free man.

All told, the arrest, trial, appeal and retrial of Archie Newton took four long years. Almost seventy witnesses were called, and countless hours were spent combing through testimony, reviewing evidence and assembling jurors. The appeal took almost two years and the retrial another twelve-plus months of waiting.

According to the *Atlanta Constitution* on December 20, 1886, the cost to the State of Florida, "from first to last," was over $30,000. This amounts to $804,000 in 2018 and represented an enormous expenditure of money, assets and prosecutorial effort.

As an aside, it does not appear that Henry Sanford attended any part of the trial or any of the preliminary hearing, the inquest or other proceedings connected to McMillan's murder. In fact, his private correspondence is devoid of any reference to McMillan's death and has little reference to Archie Newton, save for a few reports briefly mentioning the arrest or the efforts on

Archie's behalf or the trial. But even these are scant. Henry Sanford either wanted to keep out of the sordid criminal affair or did not save any letters related to the case for fear of his own reputation.

It's certainly curious that he didn't take any active role, given the fact that he was beholden to the Florida Land and Colonization Company, to Archibald Gray and to Sir William MacKinnon. Archie Newton was their nephew and had been specifically sent to Sanford's growing city on the Florida frontier. Sanford did agree to approach Gray on a trip to London in March 1883, but by the time he arrived, Gray had unexpectedly died. Sanford coldly noted this fact in a letter and continued on with his trip to Belgium.

Although he was now a free man, Archie was not out of danger, for many still believed he was guilty. After his acquittal, the *Columbus (GA) Daily Enquirer* (December 14, 1886) published the following:

> *Parties from Orange County report that it would not be healthy for Archibald William Newton, who was tried for the murder of Samuel McMillan (September 30, 1882) and acquitted last week, to parade himself in public, as he might come up missing some day.*

Archie and Kate fled Florida, never to come back.

10

THE HEADLESS MISER'S GHOST

*T*oday, the road that ran outside Sam McMillan's property—Eureka Avenue—is a four-lane divided roadway called H.E. Thomas Highway or Route 46A. It follows the same basic path as it did in 1882, but Sam, Archie Newton and none of the other characters in our story would recognize the area now.

All the orange groves are long gone, many of the gentle rolling hills have been flattened and Twin Lakes is now just the name of a housing subdivision. In fact, one of the lakes no longer even exists; it was drained so that the roadway could continue straight through rather than taking an abrupt left turn at what used to be called McMillan's Corner on Sam's property.

The spot where McMillan's orange grove once blossomed now supports a twenty-four-hour convenience store on one side and a townhouse development on the other. As you drive by, you can still see the upward slope of the land where Archie claimed he saw "Sammy's hoe" glint in the sun as he rode by on Monday, October 2, 1882.

This area is now framed in by Interstate 4. Its eight lanes cut through the once verdant meadows that Sam would have seen from the western edge of his grove as he worked.

Eureka Avenue/Route 46A passes over I-4, through three separate (and busy) shopping/dining complexes, and ends at Orange Avenue near where Coroner Edgar Harrison's store used to stand. But there are no traces left of the location of the inquest and where Kate Newton traveled on the day Sam disappeared in 1882. The area used to be called Paola, but that usage disappeared in the 1970s. It's now referred to as "Heathrow" in recognition of the large luxury housing development that sprang up in the 1980s.

The telegraph road that Archie rode his horse along to visit Zeri Adams, Pichard and Tissot, not far from Fred and Harry True, became a railroad in 1887, abandoned in the 1960s, and is now a paved walking/biking trail dotted with houses and subdivisions. None of the old houses remain.

Archie's house is long gone, as is a large part of Lake Como. The location is now part of, you guessed it, a subdivision. Much of Lake Como was either drained to make way for progress or has dried up; it is now just a small pond. Crystal Lake remains, but is far smaller, and the name now generally refers to a chain of several small lakes in the area that emerged as the larger bodies of water receded.

The unsolved murder of Samuel McMillan haunted the Twin Lakes and Sanford community for decades. Many thought that the young Englishman and his wife had gotten away with it and felt that it was wise that he fled.

As late as the 1950s, the McMillan story was still known and discussed: local historian Mary Leffler Strong specifically mentions the case in her 1950s memoir *Sanford on the St. Johns*. She included no other murder story in her book and noted that both houses were still standing at that time.

There were stories that Sam McMillan's headless corpse roamed the Twin Lakes area for years after the grisly murder. As early as November 1890, the *Atlanta Constitution* published a long article called "A Miser's Ghost." It was reported as a regular news article but included no reporter's name or attribution and cited no sources.

According to the article, it wasn't long after McMillan's death that neighbors began hearing horrible noises coming from Sam's abandoned house. There were reports of a bent-over, headless corpse walking among the orange trees as if searching for something. For over a year, people living within a radius of several miles reported seeing this ghastly corpse, which was obviously searching for its head.

Those who lived along Crystal Lake soon reported seeing a ghostly head emerge from the lake and float above the water. Some witnesses said that the stumbling corpse soon reached the lake area and would chase after the head, reaching out its decomposing limbs to try to catch it. The lengthy account of the horror explained how the head would painfully moan, "Why did they part us? Where's my body?"

The story recounts that news of this decapitated apparition and the floating head spread all over Central Florida. In 1890, having little faith in such ghost stories, a party of five men decided to investigate the case. They camped at the miser's abandoned house until dark. By midnight, nothing had happened, and the group prepared to leave.

That's when "an unearthly groan broke on their ears," and they saw a headless body, blood running down its mutilated neck, rise before them. They recognized the clothes as those of the murdered Samuel McMillan. The apparition walked around the grounds, half bent, searching for something and then made its way to the lake.

Following carefully, the horrified onlookers saw the bloody head rise up out of the dark lake. It was rotting with hideous wounds and had open, staring eyes. The headless body made a terrifying noise and ran for the head; but the head gurgled and laughed and flew out of reach. The corpse, with long, outstretched arms, raced frantically after it again and again. Each time, "impelled by an irresistible force, which it seemed unable to combat," the head moved just out of reach to torment the wild corpse.

According to the story, the five men witnessed this blood-curdling spectacle for two hours. Finally, the headless body, unable to capture its head, issued a roar of rage and ran back toward Sam's house, where it disappeared. The head returned to the pond, "where it settled down on the water and disappeared with an unearthly sound." The men fled in terror.

The men would later say that this was "the most dreadful sight they ever beheld, and that for days and nights afterward they could not get the bloody visions off their minds."

McMillan's body had been buried separately from his head, since they had been found at different times. The article notes that three of the men mustered enough courage to later dig up his head and the body and reunite them in a single coffin. This, it seems, "settled the ghost" and ended reports of the apparitions in the area.

The article seems to have originated in Tavares, Florida. You'll recall that this is the town founded by none other than prosecutor Alexander St. Clair Abrams in 1880. Since it references a location of the murder somewhere between Sanford and Tavares, and since Abrams himself was a former journalist not unfamiliar with sensationalism, it's probable that he wrote it.

The account was published as a complete story in February 1891 in a periodical called *Romance—Being the Tales of the New York Story Club*. Its title was "A Miser's Ghost. A Weird Tale of Life in Florida," and it appeared in the same edition with stories by such literary legends as Rudyard Kipling and Robert Louis Stevenson.

But once again, the story lists no author or submitting name and has no attribution. The only lead-in is the comment, "It is a fact. You can find people to-day who saw this ghost."

No other eyewitness accounts about the ghost have been uncovered. However, if true, it's not likely that the headless apparition was so easily "settled."

Sam's body was found first, as you know. It was so rotten and putrefying that it likely was immediately buried after Coroner Edgar Harrison conducted his examination on October 17, 1882. The head was found a few days later, on October 21, and by the time of trial in June 1883, it was a gleaming white skull to be passed among the jurors.

But there are no records of *where* Sam's body was buried, and there are no records of his skull *ever* being buried. Anywhere.

For all we know, Abrams or Foster kept it as a souvenir. Or perhaps some court personnel took it home or gave it away or sold it as a relic after Archie was acquitted in 1886. Or maybe it sat in a crate of other evidence accumulated by the Orange County court, forgotten on a wooden shelf in a dusty storage room.

So you see, no one could have actually dug up the head and the body as reported in the article and "reunited" them in one coffin to appease the spirit. Instead, Sam's body is still buried somewhere near Twin Lakes, and his head is still out there somewhere.

That means the ghost is still restless.

WHERE IS HE BURIED?

Sam's probate records stretch more than one hundred pages. They tell us that he died without a will and that Edgar Harrison was appointed as administrator of the estate. Eleven different heirs were identified. (Interestingly, Foster's law firm represented and took a fee from several of them.) Sam's personal possessions were sold in December 1882, netting just $49.44.

A public auction was held in December 1883 to sell his real estate. Records show that the sixteen-acre orange grove and land that Archie and Kate so desired and may have killed for eventually sold for $8,225.

As to his burial, probate records reveal that on October 17, 1882, expenses were incurred for one coffin, "expenses of a man to help," hiring of a team,

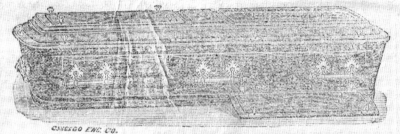

THE CELEBRATED
EMBALMING CASKET,

CSSEGO ENG. CO.

A Great Recent Invention.

Warranted to preserve the Life-like features of a body for any length of time

Chemicals with each casket, and the embalming can
be easily done by any one, instructions coming with
each case. No extra cost over the old caskets. Call and
see them.

Coffins of all Sizes constantly On hand.

Address   **P. J PARRAMORE,** Agnt for Ornge County,
Nov. 10, 1881—tf.   Or   CAPT. WM. SIRRINE, Sanford, Fla

Advertisement for casket sales by William Sirrine. *Sanford Museum Collection.*

digging a grave and paying undertaker fees. This totaled $98.00. Who coordinated the burial and received payment? William Sirrine.

But the records don't indicate where Sam's headless body was buried.

The most logical place was either the small family cemetery that J.O. Tabor had on his property or the Twin Lakes Cemetery, located about half a mile to the west of Sam's grove. Unfortunately, there are no records for either, and the latter was paved over by Rinehart Road and a car dealership in the 1990s.

It's also possible that Harrison may have interred the body at the Banana Lake Cemetery in Paola, a little closer to his store. It was situated at a small Presbyterian church on the corner where Eureka Avenue ended in Paola. But once again, records are scarce for the church and its graveyard, and attempted development in early 2000 destroyed what was left of the cemetery.

We are left, then, 135-plus years later, with more questions than answers about the final resting place of Sam McMillan.

A MYSTIC CIRCLE

Curiously, Samuel McMillan's murder and his restless ghost weren't the only mysterious murderous events to occur in this corner of Sanford, Florida. In fact, there are several instances of murder and unexplained death in this area throughout the 1880s and 1890s.

Perhaps as a harbinger of things to come, the town of Paola had a theatrical performance group called "The Mystics." The July 26, 1883 edition of the *Sanford Journal* noted that at a recent performance, one of the stage lamps flared up suddenly and with no cause as to why. The flame then ran down into the bowl of the lamp and was "blazing all over." The crowd panicked, as it seemed that the entire stage would burn, when the Mystics director "very bravely and coolly" picked it up and threw it outside before further mayhem ensued.

This would-be conflagration occurred just a week after Newton was found guilty of murder in 1883. There is, of course, no connection between the Mystics and Archie or McMillan, but it is a curious name to consider given the mystical ghost story that was starting to be told about the Headless Miser. It's also curious when we consider the host of dark and mysterious happenings in the Twin Lakes/Paola area.

In late October 1885, a man named C.L. Sims disappeared one night while walking home from his sister's house in Paola. Local papers called it "As Profound a Mystery as Ever." A few of the men who searched for Sam McMillan found themselves searching again for another missing person just three years later. Sims's lifeless body was soon found floating in the Wekiva River.

The coroner's inquest and the initial autopsy revealed nothing conclusive. But foul play was suspected, and as before, "There was great dissatisfaction among the people." This was just three years after McMillan's disappearance and murder, and newspaper accounts noted that the people "are fully roused and the officers are on the alert."

None other than Zeri Adams played a key role in the Sims investigation as part of the inquest. The body was later exhumed so that a second autopsy could be performed. It revealed that the left rib over the heart had been broken, which was a similar finding to McMillan's body (the first left rib and collarbone had been broken). The second Sims autopsy also showed no water in the lungs, leading to the conclusion that Sims had been killed before entering the water.

Despite the unrest of the citizenry, the exact cause of his death was never found, and no one was arrested for his murder. Archie Newton must have read about this event as he sat in jail, waiting for his retrial, and may have wondered if he would somehow be blamed for Sims's death as well.

In 1893, Paola resident Annie Ballsley shot her husband, J.H. Ballsley, while he slept. She stayed in the house with his corpse for two days before shooting herself in their bedroom.

The Ballsleys were among the earliest settlers of the Paola area, arriving in 1873. They built a successful orange grove that bordered on the telegraph road that Archie knew well; maps show that their tract of land was larger than many in the area. Their house looked south over their expanse of orange trees, and they likely would have been able to see the houses of Pichard, Fred True and Zeri Adams, with Harrison's store in the distance.

No motive was ever discerned for Annie Ballsley's murder-suicide, and talk of the house being haunted was not long in coming.

Several other mysterious deaths, disappearances and suicides plagued this area for many years. If you draw a circle around this roughly two-mile area, you encapsulate most of the locations of these dark events. If we use Paola's performance group as a naming convention, you have the Mystic Circle.

This Mystic Circle intersects with the portion of Interstate 4 identified as the "I-4 Deadzone." This section of the highway is just past Twin Lakes and Paola heading east, and it is legendary for the high number of traffic accidents and unexplained incidents that occur on a very short stretch of road. Motorists claim that cellphones don't work when driving through, and static interferes with car radios. A few have reported seeing "wispy balls of light that zigzag just above the pavement."

Locals blame the desecration of a small cemetery plot when the highway was built in 1960. Newspapers run stories with headlines such as "Do Paved-Over Souls Haunt I-4?" and "High Number of I-4 Traffic Accidents Baffle Officials." Ghost hunters stop and take pictures, and people often inquire at the Sanford Museum about the best viewing spot. Whether paranormal or not, this area certainly has a peculiar air to it, much like the macabre goings-on of nearby Twin Lakes.

Although Sam's body is buried somewhere in the Mystic Circle, we don't know where. But since we know it has never been united with his head, Samuel McMillan remains the Headless Miser.

BIBLIOGRAPHY

"An Illustrious Founder." Lake & Sumter Style—City Feature Series, September 1, 2013. Accessed June 2, 2017. https://www. lakeandsumterstyle.com/city-series-tavares-americas-seaplane-city.

Archibald W. Newton v. The State of Florida (June Term 1884). Cases Argued and Adjudged in the Supreme Court of Florida During the Years 1884-5-6. Tallahassee, FL: Floridian Book and Job Office, 1886.

Blackman, William Fremont. *History of Orange County, Florida Narrative and Biographical*. Orlando, FL: E.O. Painter Printing, 1927.

Carlson, Charlie. *Weird Florida*. New York: Sterling Publishing, 2005.

Chase Collection, Special and Area Studies Collections. George A. Smathers Libraries, University of Florida, Gainesville, Florida.

Church of England—Births and Baptisms 1813–1906: Archibald William Newton. Ancestry.com interactive. Accessed May 15, 2017. https://www. ancestry.com/interactive/Print/1558/31280_199161-00221/5685288.

"Dade County Courthouse." Hidden History Miami. Accessed August 12, 2017. http://hiddenhistorymiami.com/dang-2.html.

Florida, State Census, 1885—Orange, District Orlando. FLM845_10-0027. Ancestry.com. Accessed July 10, 2017.

Foster, Eleazar Kingsbury. Yale Obituary Record. Manuscripts and Archives. Yale University Library, 1899. New Haven, Connecticut.

Fry, Joseph. *Diplomacy and Business in Nineteenth Century America*. Reno: University of Nevada Press, 1982.

Henry Shelton Sanford Papers. Sanford Museum, Sanford, Florida.

History of the Orange County Jail System—Orange County Jail #1 (1873–1884). The Orange County Regional History Center, 1983. Orlando Florida.

Images of Yale Individuals. RU 684. Manuscripts and Archives. Yale University Library. New Haven, Connecticut.

Letters from E.R. Trafford to Henry Shelton Sanford. February 10, 1883, May 12, 1883. Henry Shelton Sanford Collection. Sanford Museum, Sanford, Florida.

MacKinnon, Sir William, 1ˢᵗ Baronet. Ref. Code GB 0102 PP MS 1. School of Oriental and African Studies. Accessed July 2, 2017. http://www.aim25.ac.uk/cgi-bin/frames/fulldesc?inst_id=19&coll_id=149.

McMillan, Samuel. In the Matter of the Estate of. Orange County Florida—Court of County Judge, As A Court of Probate. FamilySearch.org. Accessed January 15, 2017.

Munro, J. Forbes. *Maritime Enterprise and Empire: Sir William MacKinnon and His Business Network, 1823–1893.* Rochester, NY: Boydell Press, 2003.

Newton v. N.W. Provinces (High Court of). XIV Moore Ind. App. 267, 1871. Mews' Digital. INDIA; 3. Legal Decisions.

Newton, Anne MacKinnon (born Gray). MyHeritage Family Trees. MyHeritage. Accessed July 2, 2017. https://www.myheritage.com/research/record-1-436471221-1-3250/a.

Newton, Thomas. MyHeritage Family Trees. MyHeritage. Accessed July 2, 2017. https://www.myheritage.com/research/record-1-436471221-1-3249/th.

New York, Passenger Lists, 1820–1957. M237, Roll 438 (NYM237_438-1117). Ancestry.com. Accessed July 10, 2017.

Research and Archive Collection (various). Museum of Seminole County History, Lake Mary, Florida.

Robbins, H. Franklin, and Steven G. Mason. *A Retrospective Look at the Orange County Circuit Criminal Court and Its Judges Between 1847 and 1876.* http://www.sgmason.com/sgmarticles/judges.htm.

———. *A Retrospective Look at the Prosecutors of the Orange County Circuit Criminal Court Between 1847 and 1884.* http://www.sgmason.com/sgmarticles/prosecutors.htm.

Robison, Jim. "James Ingraham Was the Man behind 3 Tycoons." *Orlando Sentinel*, May 10, 1992.

Romance—Being the Tales of the New York Story Club. February 1891. Google books online, accessed 2017.

Roth, Michael P. *Historical Dictionary of War Journalism.* Westport, CT: Greenwood Press, 1997.

State of Florida v. Archibald W. Newton. Trial Transcript (1883). S 49. State Archives of Florida.

"St. Clair Abrams, Alexander H." Revolvy Topics. Accessed August 12, 2017. https://www.revolvy.com/topic/Alexander%20St.%20Clair-Abrams&uid=1575.

Strong, Mary Leffler. *Sanford on the St. John's*. Unpublished manuscript, 1950.

United States Federal Census (1900). San Francisco, California, District 0013. Ancestry.com.

Waitley, Douglas. *Best Backroads of Florida. The Heartland*. Vol. 1. Sarasota, FL: Pineapple Press, 2006.

INDEX

A

Abrams, Alexander St. Clair 14,
   98, 102, 105, 107, 109, 110,
   111, 113, 114, 115, 116, 117,
   118, 119, 121, 122, 124, 125,
   129, 130, 131, 136, 137, 138,
   139, 140, 142, 143, 144, 150,
   152, 153, 154, 155, 159, 160
Adams, Zeri 68, 72, 73, 74, 75, 76,
   80, 87, 88, 90, 93, 98, 158,
   162, 163

B

Beardall, William 66, 95
blood, evidence 95, 138, 139, 140,
   141, 142, 143, 148
Bowron, Pollie 30, 31, 32, 33, 34,
   35, 36, 37, 38, 43, 132, 147

C

Caldwell, Dr. F. A. 114, 115, 136
Cocke, Judge W. Arthur 107, 108,
   109, 110, 121, 140, 143, 144,
   150, 153, 154
coroner 91, 92, 126, 162
Crystal Lake 70, 71, 72, 88, 97,
   114, 123, 147, 158

D

DeForest, Henry 21, 22, 42, 43, 46

E

Eureka Avenue 43, 46, 59, 157

F

Florida Land and Colonization
   Company 25, 29, 110, 156

Foster, Eleazar K., Jr. 14, 104, 105, 108, 109, 110, 116, 118, 119, 122, 124, 125, 128, 131, 134, 140, 141, 142, 143, 144, 150, 151, 153, 154, 155, 160

Fox, Tony 83, 85, 89, 92, 95, 97, 118, 125

G

ghost story 157

gold ring, evidence 95, 130

Gray, Archibald 25, 26, 29, 43, 156

Grohman, John (gunsmith) 120, 121, 122

H

hair, evidence 55, 97, 116, 141, 142, 143, 148

Harrison, Edgar 71, 72, 79, 83, 84, 87, 88, 89, 91, 92, 93, 94, 95, 124, 125, 130, 138, 157, 160, 161, 163

head, severed 89, 96, 97, 114, 116, 136, 137, 138, 147, 158, 159, 160, 163

I

Ingraham, James 16, 39, 41, 42, 46, 47, 49, 65, 66, 67, 73, 87, 95, 98, 150, 151

J

Jones, Ellen 32, 33, 34, 35, 36, 37, 38, 132, 154, 155

jury 13, 16, 58, 64, 71, 72, 93, 94, 99, 100, 102, 107, 108, 109, 110, 111, 113, 115, 116, 119, 120, 121, 129, 139, 144, 147, 148, 150, 154, 155, 160

L

Lake Como 43, 72, 84, 88, 89, 92, 96, 97, 124, 158

Lake Monroe 17, 20, 21, 22, 43

London, England 16, 25, 27, 28, 30, 31, 32, 34, 35, 36, 37, 38, 43, 65, 132, 149, 156

M

MacKinnon, Sir William 25, 26, 29, 31, 35, 65, 99, 156

McMillan, Samuel 13, 14, 16, 26, 46, 49, 50, 52, 54, 55, 58, 60, 61, 62, 63, 64, 65, 66, 67, 68, 70, 72, 73, 74, 75, 76, 77, 78, 79, 80, 81, 82, 83, 84, 85, 86, 87, 88, 92, 93, 96, 97, 98, 107, 109, 111, 113, 114, 122, 123, 124, 126, 127, 129, 130, 131, 132, 135, 136, 138, 142, 143, 147, 148, 152, 155, 156, 157, 158, 159, 161, 162, 163

McRae, T.M. 132, 133

Middlemas, Andrew 65

Miller, Leslie 58, 62

miser. *See* McMillan, Samuel

Moore, Lindley 59, 82, 87, 88, 95, 98

Munson, Eugene 77, 78, 80

Mystic Circle 162, 163

N

Newton, Anne 29
Newton, Archibald 13, 14, 16, 18,
    26, 27, 28, 29, 30, 31, 32, 33,
    34, 35, 36, 37, 38, 39, 41, 42,
    43, 46, 47, 49, 50, 57, 58, 59,
    61, 63, 64, 65, 66, 67, 68, 70,
    71, 72, 73, 74, 75, 76, 77, 78,
    79, 80, 82, 83, 84, 85, 86, 87,
    88, 89, 90, 92, 93, 94, 95, 96,
    97, 98, 99, 100, 101, 102,
    104, 105, 107, 108, 109, 110,
    111, 113, 114, 117, 119, 120,
    123, 124, 125, 126, 127, 130,
    131, 132, 133, 134, 137, 138,
    141, 142, 143, 144, 147, 149,
    150, 151, 152, 153, 154, 155,
    156, 157, 158, 160, 162, 163
Newton, Kate 14, 30, 31, 32, 33,
    35, 36, 37, 38, 43, 47, 61, 64,
    65, 67, 71, 72, 73, 75, 76, 82,
    85, 86, 93, 96, 98, 101, 109,
    113, 114, 117, 123, 127, 130,
    132, 133, 147, 148, 151, 152,
    155, 156, 157, 160
Newton, Thomas 28, 29

O

Orange County 65, 82, 86, 92, 94,
    98, 100, 102, 108, 144, 147,
    155, 156, 160
Orange County Courthouse 102,
    103, 104, 107
Orange County Jail 31, 98, 99,
    100, 102, 105, 144, 147, 155,
    163

orange grove 39, 49, 52, 74, 77, 98,
    111, 113, 148, 157, 160, 163
Orlando 13, 17, 42, 52, 65, 92, 99,
    101, 102, 103, 104, 105, 122,
    134

P

Paola 50, 78, 79, 91, 92, 104, 157,
    161, 162, 163
Pichard, A. 61, 67, 73, 74, 76, 77,
    79, 80, 81, 85, 87, 125, 126,
    127, 128, 133, 158, 163
pot of nails, evidence 98

S

Saint, Charles 54, 58, 60, 70, 73,
    80, 85, 86, 87, 116, 129, 142,
    143
Salem, OH 52, 58, 130
Sanford, FL 16, 17, 39, 81, 83,
    132, 162
Sanford, Henry 19, 20, 24, 25, 39,
    41, 42, 43, 59, 66, 98, 99,
    102, 103, 105, 110, 111, 150,
    156
Sanford Journal 65, 75, 94, 134, 143,
    162
Shine, T. W. (sherriff) 92, 102, 107,
    109, 110, 111, 130, 147
Sirrine, William 92, 94, 95, 96, 98,
    114, 115, 118, 119, 120, 121,
    122, 123, 126, 129, 130, 138,
    139, 161
South Florida Journal 64, 83, 93, 94,
    152
Stewart, Mrs. Francis 70, 72, 73
St. John's River 17, 20

T

Tabor, J.O. 57, 58, 60, 66, 67, 70,
        73, 80, 81, 82, 87, 95, 113,
        142, 143, 161
Tissot, Emile 65, 75, 95, 158
True, Fred 75, 86, 98, 111, 117,
        121, 122, 123, 125, 147, 148,
        158, 163
True, Harry 75, 111, 158
Twin Lakes, FL 20, 22, 42, 43, 50,
        52, 61, 72, 81, 92, 99, 104,
        157, 158, 160, 161, 162, 163

W

wallet, evidence 60, 78
Wilson, Thomas 14, 83, 92, 93, 95,
        96, 98, 153
Woodson, J.H. 79, 96, 97, 114